Praise for *Creator to Com*

"Working with Deb was a lovely journey. The name 'Find Calm Here' 100 percent fits what Deb does. She entered into the conversation with a calm attitude. In a month, I went from being frustrated and not knowing what to do— to being calm and confident in building, growing, and working inside my network. She knows her stuff!"
— Robin Fuller

"Deb Schell is a master at Community Building & Membership Design. She is an excellent listener, communicator, and systems strategist keeping her clients' passion, vision, and end users in mind throughout her community design process."
— Carol Dockum

"Deb takes something that feels overwhelming and simply settles you into a foundation. She has this ability to keep you focusing on your North Star while at the same time creating space for the unknown. She is brilliant and calm, and we couldn't have done this without her."
— Sarah Hines

"I feel like I found the golden ticket when I found Deb. I love Deb's strategic thinking and teaching style. Deb has a wonderful sense of humor and made me feel so comfortable. I HIGHLY recommend working with Deb when you are ready to grow."
— Lisa Pepper-Satkin

"One of the things I love best about Deb is that she personi-
fies her motto, 'Find Calm Here.' When she was referred
to me, I was overwhelmed with the sheer volume of work
needed to launch my community. She took control of the
situation, like a seasoned senior project manager, focused
on the low-hanging fruit that needed to be prioritized,
and rolled up her sleeves and helped where needed. As a
result, everything was accomplished AHEAD of the deadline. It made me feel very CALM. I highly recommend Deb
if you're looking to launch a community and need expertise, project support, strategy, and guidance."

— *Tiana Clark*

Creator to Community Builder

Creator to *Community Builder*

Find Calm While Building Your Online Community

DEB SCHELL

Photos by Deb Schell
Edited by Suzi Hunn and Danielle Anderson
Cover and book design by Paul Nylander

ISBN 979-8-9888166-0-7 (softcover); 979-8-9888166-1-4 (ePub)
Library of Congress Control Number: 2023916686

To order this book in bulk quantities, please contact Deb Schell via email at Deb@FindCalmHere.com for discounted rates on ten or more copies for your team.

Go to bonus.creator2communitybuilder.com for downloadable resources.

For my niece, Emilia, and my nephew, Joseph.

For my best friend, Jeanette. Tag! It's your turn to write a book!

For the next generation of leaders to create communities that offer members a sense of belonging, connection, and an opportunity for all human beings to be seen, heard, and valued.

For the wild ones who refuse to simply follow the traditional path and want to carve a new trail that fits their ideal lifestyle.

For the Find Calm Here community founding members who helped build the foundational content of this book.

For the future creators, dynamic leaders, and innovative thinkers.

For the communities that will lead change, develop compassion for others, and embrace a new era of learning, connection, and social justice.

For the struggling community builders who know they have something to teach and want to share their life's work, learned experiences, and wisdom with future generations.

For creators who want to enjoy the community-building process by co-creating—with their ideal members—a community culture that inspires safety, vulnerability, and transformation.

For my past, present, and future clients to have on your desks as your guide because community building is an ever-changing journey.

Table of Contents

Introduction I

Section 1: Community Purpose, Strategy, Structure 7
    Chapter 1: Learn the Community—Building Basics 9
    Chapter 2: Develop Your Community Strategy 27
    Chapter 3: Explore Your Community Design and Structure 43

Section 2: Ideal Members, Validation, Planning 77
    Chapter 4: Discover Your Ideal Members 79
    Chapter 5: Validate Your Community 93
    Chapter 6: Plan Your Community. 101

Section 3: Building, Launching, and Onboarding 109
    Chapter 7: Grow Your Audience 111
    Chapter 8: Launch Your Community 123
    Chapter 9: Onboard Your Members . .. .139

Section 4: Community Retention, Growth, and Maintenance 151
    Chapter 10: Keep Members Coming Back 153
    Chapter 11: Grow Your Membership. 163
    Chapter 12: Maintain Your Community 173

Afterward: So, What's Next? 183
Acknowledgements 187
About the Author 189

Mt. Sniktau, Loveland, Colorado

"I would rather walk with a friend in the dark than alone in the light."

— *Helen Keller*

Introduction

Peace, calm, and awe are what I discovered near the summit of Colorado's Mount Sniktau. My trip to the mountain wasn't just for "fun"; it was part of the new career I was building as a travel writer and photographer. I was determined to explore calm destinations to build a niche in the travel industry.

This new business pursuit led me to an online community that would change my life and transform my career in ways I never could have imagined. The group is called Location Indie, and it caters to professionals like me who are passionate about travel and working remotely. I joined soon after finding them. It only took speaking with a few members to know I'd found "my people." I felt as though they understood me and the life I dreamed of. I yearned to travel while pitching stories, taking photographs, and writing. Ultimately, my experience with this community would inspire a completely different career path.

The community was hosting an in-person workshop in Denver, Colorado, and I was one of the first to sign up and book my flight. I'd never been to Colorado and, until that opportunity, had never even considered going. Once I arrived and met these fantastic people, I knew this was the life I wanted, but I still didn't know how to make it happen.

What made this community unique was that they were so diverse; they came together from all over the world to support each other. We didn't simply talk about developing online businesses; we actively pursued them, and when we dreamed of a location-independent lifestyle, we didn't feel alone.

A few months after that event, the community offered a trip to Central Mexico focused on identifying a side hustle, which was right up my alley. Not only did it offer that, but it also featured a workshop on travel writing! I was thrilled with the prospect of reconnecting with these amazing people, so I grabbed my passport and was on my way.

The trip was magical, but understanding the "how" of being a travel writer was a struggle. I was given the feedback that I needed to decide on a niche to pitch stories to editors. I spent hours talking with fellow community members who encouraged and challenged me to brainstorm alternative ways to make money. During a walk with friends at a monarch butterfly sanctuary, Santuario de la Mariposa Monarca El Rosario, I realized that I wanted to focus my writing on destinations of calm in the upcoming chapter of my life.

My life was far from calm at the time. I worked a corporate sales job for a large distribution company in Central Pennsylvania, and while it paid the bills, it didn't bring me joy. In fact, it brought anxiety, stress, and frustration. However, I needed the money. I'd spent ten years trying to make a living as a creator and had ended up with over $45,000 of debt.

At the time, I'd been listening to a podcast called *Achieve Your Goals with Hal Elrod*. He is the author of *The Miracle Morning*, a book that changed my perspective on how to start a side hustle while still working in a nine-to-five job. His book is all about building the life you want using only one hour in the morning.

In one episode, he mentioned hosting a virtual call with some of his colleagues and invited listeners to join him in a conversation with Jon Berghoff, creator of the XChange program. This collaborative learning community has brought together more than 500 coaches and trainers from around the world. I was intrigued!

During the session, Jon explained how he'd transitioned to virtual coaching programs during the pandemic. This approach aligned with my wish for location independence, so I took him up on his offer for a free session, no strings attached. On this call, Jon and I chatted about a passion project I'd been running on the side. To support my mission to help others find calm, I'd been hosting in-person events that explored ways to address the depression and anxiety I'd experienced in my own life.

Encouraged by my mission, Jon explained how I could create a virtual transformational experience. Using prompts and breakout rooms, I could cultivate conversations that would create a sense of belonging, safety, and joy. Inspired, I set up my first virtual event, a workshop about essential oils. Eight people showed up, so I considered the effort a success.

After that experience, I became more serious about exploring the world of online communities and memberships. I started with reaching out to new community builders and taking a course on how to build an online community. There was so much to consider, but the thought of being able to host workshops and be paid for it had me thinking that this was a dream job with real potential.

Still wanting to figure out how to work for myself, I decided to launch a wellness community to expand my efforts with helping people find calm in daily life. I envisioned a thriving group like Location Indie. I started paying attention to what community builders were saying about how to launch a community on one's own. Based on advice I frequently saw on social media, I planned a single launch day preceded by a ton of content.

Along the way, I learned about sales funnels, branding, and video editing, and I met several other community builders, many whom I welcomed into my new community. To promote my community, I decided to launch a four-hour virtual summit featuring fifteen speakers. Based on the model I was taught, I created social media accounts, began posting all about who the community was for and what we were going to do, and offered it as a free experience—up until launch day—to all who wanted to try it. I planned a schedule for the rest of the year, including talks from experts in breathwork, self-care, and mindset.

Despite all the action I had taken, I watched my dream come to a screeching halt when I attracted *zero* paid members by the end of the launch. I felt like a failure; I thought I'd done everything right. Even more, the experience was anxiety-inducing and frustrating.

I would learn later that although I'd failed to achieve my stated goal, I'd unwittingly succeeded at something else. Remember the community builders I'd invited into my space? We still enjoyed each other's camaraderie, so much so that we continued to meet weekly. I noticed myself waking up on the mornings of our calls feeling excited to connect. By supporting them through challenges, some have even become friends.

They asked me questions, leaned in when I answered, and told me that I was "meant to do this kind of work." One of them asked to discuss her community. By the end of the call, she said, "Deb, you've helped me figure out things I've been trying to figure out for months; you should get paid to do this!" It was then that I discovered the career path that sustains me to this day—helping fellow community builders.

One of my early consulting calls was focused on helping a client craft their community strategy, and afterward, I felt as though I had finally found my purpose. It is a feeling that can only be understood by those who have experienced it. There are no words to describe it other than to say I cried tears of joy. As word got around, I became a go-to for community builders who needed extra support for their upcoming projects.

Since officially launching my business in 2020, I've helped over sixty entrepreneurs build, launch, and grow their businesses with an online community. Some of my clients have a team, but not all of them do. Some have existing businesses; others don't. I've worked with individuals in Canada, Mexico, Europe, the United Kingdom, Australia, New Zealand, and the United States. My twenty years of experience as a writer, creator, and designer has allowed me to create a business that helps leaders, creatives, entrepreneurs, speakers, authors, and executives take the guesswork out of community building.

Most new community builders struggle to launch because they are overwhelmed with the technology, aren't clear about who they serve, or want to scale their businesses but don't know how. This means they miss out on making money they could have charged had they launched faster, grown sooner, and created bigger transformations for their members.

I don't want you to miss out, too. This book will help you take action sooner and create an additional revenue stream for your business. It will not be easy, but I've compiled all the resources and guidance you'll need to make your journey as simple as possible. Hopefully, they will also bring you calm, joy, and ease.

SECTION 1:

Community Purpose, Strategy, Structure

Querétaro, Mexico

> *"No one remains committed to a community if it doesn't help them grow into who they want to be . . . you must ensure they have a way to grow."*
>
> — *Carrie Melissa Jones*

CHAPTER 1

Learn the Community— Building Basics

Because of the global pandemic, the world had to adjust to living in a bubble and withdrawing from in-person social connections. I don't know about you, but the events of those years shifted my perspective on how I spend my time. Most people I've talked with have shared that they've enjoyed exploring their hobbies, spending increased time with loved ones, and building new relationships with their peers who have similar values, challenges, and goals.

Trends such as the great resignation and quiet quitting ultimately stemmed from the awareness that each of us has a limited time on Earth. For some, that means rethinking personal lifestyle goals. Many of us have looked at how the life we're currently living stacks up to our ideal life. Noticing the distance between where we want to be and where we really are makes an impact. We start to question what is true, and each person may answer differently.

* Are there only some people who get to enjoy life?
* How can I choose happiness when I'm always working so hard to find it?
* Why do I need to accept the world's version of what is right for me?
* Why do I need to find some other path to be successful simply because the world doesn't value my work in a financial sense?
* Why am I working at this company if they can fire me at any moment?
* What's the point of working for someone else's dream when I can make my own dream a reality? How do I do that? I can't figure it out, so I give up!
* Should I be married by the time I'm thirty-five years old?
* Do I need to have children to be happy?

I'm sharing a gift that was given to me, a quote I often remind myself of:

"Comparison is the thief of joy."
— *Theodore Roosevelt*

If you grew up without siblings, you have had a different experience than someone who didn't. If you grew up with siblings, each of you had a different experience with your parental figures. Some people have lived in poverty all of their lives and have no idea what it's like to live in a world where their needs are met.

Some have lived through trauma, stress, and drama and act like it's just another week, then wonder why their bodies hurt.

Since social media has become such a huge presence in our lives, it has become difficult to understand how our lives *should* look compared to what we see when scrolling. Social media is flooded with thousands of perfect family photos or impeccable food images in destinations that some of us may never be able to afford. It has led many of us to feel we are not enough and has caused us to focus on hustling to start doing our own thing because we haven't found peace or satisfaction at work.

That is why many new online communities offer virtual events, master classes, and networking opportunities to replace traditional local meetups. These new communities give people—those looking to expand their awareness about different ways of working—the opportunity to connect with others worldwide.

With this new technological capability comes the responsibility to be an active participant in the community because a community is an ecosystem and is only as strong as its members. There are thousands of online communities you can join today to learn a new skill, meet new people, or share common interests.

If you have decided to start a community because you discovered, like me, how wonderful it is to be in a group of individuals who share the same values, have the same problems, and support each other, you have embarked upon a unique challenge to identify your ideal members and validate that they want to be in an online community.

Creators are shifting their focus from passive income to purposeful content. Since I began working on becoming more mindful and intentional about my life, I've noticed there are two movements happening in the creator economy.

The first is a term you're probably familiar with—hustle culture—which has blossomed out of the need for constant content creation. Creators are searching for brands to partner with for sponsorship and advertising revenue. Content creators know they can create great content, but they don't know how to monetize it.

One of the traditional ways creators monetized their content included affiliate marketing or brand ambassadorship. These ambassadors are now called influencers. Bloggers, marketers, and social media creators monetize their content by leveraging their large audiences to broker brand deals.

What I've learned is that it is easier to work with smaller groups of people and charge $1,000, rather than trying to sell thousands of

$10 units (memberships, courses, programs) every day, month, or year. However, if you aren't going to build an audience of 100,000 people, how do you become profitable as a community builder or membership site? Find your purpose.

Your Community Needs Purpose

We've all heard stats about how many people are online; more importantly, many people who regularly engage online are also looking to make connections. According to an article by PeerBoard, seventy-six percent of internet users were projected to participate in some type of online community in 2022. Over 2.9 billion people are reported to be active on Facebook, which is home to more than 10 million groups; chances are likely that the majority of those nearly three billion users are in at least one group. On Reddit, there are more than 130,000 active communities, mainly in the United States.

Though these stats demonstrate there are more ways than ever to connect digitally with others, the sheer volume of opportunities doesn't necessarily mean people feel an increased sense of belonging. All too often, people still feel isolated, as though they don't have a voice. As a community builder, establishing your purpose is critical to ensure your members feel they belong and will be heard.

The vision of your community may change over time, but having a clear purpose when you begin will be vital to your success. In this chapter, I'll outline the basics of online community building and explain the difference between an audience and a community. The chapter will end with some action steps to start you moving in the right direction.

What is an Online Community?

Google "what is an online community," and you may find a variety of answers. To make sure we're on the same page throughout this book, here's my baseline definition: an online community is a group of three or more people with similar ambitions who gather virtually to inspire each other through content, experiences, and encouragement.

There are three important elements of an online community:

1. A place to meet digitally to be seen, heard, and valued
2. A routine, habit, or ritual community members do together
3. A common challenge, goal, desire, or need

Online communities can congregate in many different places and ways. Here are a few examples:

* A single virtual call that offers members a space to connect
* An email that is shared with more than three people
* A forum, chat room, or group text that allows people to share photos, videos, audios, or other content
* A platform that invites a specific group of people into a private online place for connection, collaboration, and conversations
* A virtual event that offers attendees an opportunity to meet, network, connect, and discuss topics related to the event's focus, themes, or educational content

The Platform is Not the Community; the People Are

The first question many new community builders ask me is, "What's the best platform for my community?" My response is always that it's not only about the tools, but it's also about how you intend to use them.

Before jumping into a launch plan and committing to a platform, put down your checklists and pause to think about what brought you to community building in the first place.

I've seen my community-building clients become stuck with comparing the latest and greatest technology before considering the community's purpose. Their focus is on quickly generating revenue, which leads them to buy into a platform's claims about how easy community building can be.

As busy entrepreneurs juggling many things, it's easy to think that finding the right system will kick things off fast. However, when putting software first, many rookie community builders forget to consider their members.

A community is a group of humans with unpredictably busy and full lives. People aren't transactions; they have thoughts, feelings, and needs. No matter where people gather, *they* are the community—the place is irrelevant. The key to building a thriving community is to focus on the right *p*—people—rather than profits or platform.

Are You Building an Audience or an Online Community?

In a world where "community" has become a buzzword applied to just about every nook and cranny of the internet, you may, rightfully, be confused about what this word means when applied to your business. To help shed some light on this, I'll share examples of communities, ways to build them, and what makes them successful.

Before we go too far, though, I want to make one thing clear. Building a community isn't the same as building an audience. In fact, I often say you need to build an audience *before* you can form a community. The key difference is you send one-way messages to your audience, but a community talks to each other collaboratively.

Look closely at how I've defined these terms here:

☆ **Audience**: People who follow or buy from a business that communicates with them through one-directional messages

☆ **Community**: A group of people who can communicate with each other

To build an audience, you create content that is then advertised to your current customers or followers. Maybe you use an email list, host a podcast, or run a YouTube channel. Either way, these are all examples of one-way communication. An email list, podcast audience, or group of YouTube viewers aren't a community. Instead, think of a community as an intentional group meeting for a specific purpose.

Another important point is that a social media platform is *not the same as a community platform*. Social media platforms exist as a means for people to create and share content. Content shared on social media is often created to serve a business need (marketing, advertising, etc.), but a community helps its members meet *their* needs. When built and maintained intentionally, communities create *calm*. Consider the last time you logged onto Facebook, LinkedIn, or Twitter. If you're anything like me, the experience usually brings distraction or comparison, not calm.

According to Hivebrite, a community platform, social media isn't ideal for community building. In fact, they say communities built *off* of social media provide fewer distractions and less spam. When you choose a place to run your community that's dedicated to your sole purpose, it "facilitates authentic self-expression and a feeling of belonging. Members are more likely to reach out to share ideas, opinions, and best practices, ask and answer questions, and take action."

Another reason to avoid building a community on common social media platforms is that you have little control over the experience. When Facebook and Instagram went down for several hours in October 2021, many business owners were dealt a gut punch.

"While the IG outage was mildly stressful, it did reaffirm some of the concerns . . . Namely, that IG rarely rewards us for the time we invest and that relying on a third party to mediate our relationships with customers is risky business," said Rachel Jones, founder of Jonesey.

Of course, all online communities rely on technology to work effectively. However, social media platforms can remove, delete, copy, or take ownership of any content created on their platforms. This is why I encourage you to consider hosting a community on a platform other than social media.

The Pursuit of Passive Income

When I started this journey, I kept hearing how easy it is to build an online community. These messages from community platforms and industry leaders pushed the ideas of passive income and how a community "runs itself."

Reality check. Since working with—and interviewing—dozens of community builders, I've discovered that those who found quick and easy success already had a team and had built an audience over time, often up to a decade. It was no overnight victory!

In an enlightening conversation, author and business coach Pamela Slim shared two ways to think of your community as you build it. One is to see it as "building an empire." This more hierarchical approach portrays a community's leadership as an all-knowing authority. The other way—the perspective she and I prefer—is to see your community as an ecosystem. As is the case in nature, all the parts within your ecosystem play an important role. Each part helps the others grow.

In my early days, I based my online community launch on a model I'd seen work for others. However, those people had built their communities with existing audiences I did not have. I didn't have an email list, a social media presence, or a podcast with thousands of listeners. I didn't have a business list, client list, or any kind of existing program, course, or guide for my potential members. They had no idea who I was, what the community was really about, and how it could help them.

So, the first problem I encountered as a new community builder was I had learned a system that was designed for individuals who *did* have an audience and planned to build a community with sales funnels, email marketing, and courses or workshops.

In lieu of an audience, I built my network by leveraging other peoples' audiences, asking them to promote this community for me, and giving them a partnership' with my new business from which they would be able to benefit financially if they brought their audiences to my community.

This ultimately failed because the partners I onboarded into the program already had their own businesses and were struggling to gain their own clients, customers, or audiences.

I promoted others for six months, and by the end of the year, I was burnt out and exhausted. After spending almost $5,000 and hours of time, energy, and effort, I had nothing financial to show for it. The notion that anyone can quickly build an online community and make a living off it is unrealistic and, in my opinion, dangerous.

The Power of Community as an Ecosystem

In the context of community building, an ecosystem model encourages community members to share and support each other, recognizing we all have value. There's no authority figure who has all the answers. Instead, there's a facilitator who helps guide individuals during challenging times. This is the kind of community I want to be a part of, and it's the kind I encourage you to build.

A community based on shared wisdom means that while a host provides the education, tools, and resources, the ultimate goal is for members to share how they are implementing what they've learned.

The challenge—and the joy—of building an ecosystem is that you'll need to work extensively with ideal members right from the beginning. You'll need to seek out founding (or beta) members to pinpoint a common problem they face.

From there, having gained firsthand information from your founding members, you will be able to develop valuable content and experiences that actually address the issues at hand. This could include books, courses, or coaching around a specific topic. When positing this to members, it should be clear the focus is to help them. If your concept isn't well developed, your process may require serving the group for a low cost—or even free—until you figure out how best to meet their needs.

Showing the value of community is a complex challenge. So many companies understand the idea behind having a community, but they don't know how to reap the financial benefits. Many new community builders I work with want to launch their community as a paid offer before they've validated their concepts.

To promote *The Community Strategy Podcast* and find new clients, I spoke at a conference in Orlando called Podfest, specifically intended for podcasters. During my five-minute talk, I shared the benefits of talking to ideal community members before launching an online community.

Afterward, I was approached by a woman who wanted to speak with me about her community concept. She mentioned she had an active Facebook community, and she planned to launch a paid daily motivational podcast as an offer to members. "Do you think I can convert members to this private daily motivational podcast?" she asked me.

I let that sink in and responded, "That sounds like a lot of work. Did they ask you for a daily motivational podcast?" She looked at me and said, "Deb, they didn't, but I thought they'd want it." I told her it would be more important to ask them first and validate it before she started building. She thanked me for saving her a lot of time, energy, and money and preventing a situation that could have led her to feel as though she'd failed, simply because she didn't ask her members what they wanted.

If you're considering building an online community, let's talk about the elephant in the room. With so many options, where do you start? What if you're new to the digital world? Whether you're a founder or team member, this book will provide stories to inspire you, offer challenges you can relate to, and give you hope for finding a path that fits your needs while still honoring your members' shared wisdom.

What's Your Why?

Some of my clients fear they don't have what it takes to build a community. They think they can't begin without a certification, degree, or accreditation. If you feel this way, let me tell you what I tell them: none of this is as important as knowing your *why*.

Sure, your reasoning is likely financial, and you certainly have business goals. For example, some leaders start an online community to offer resources in one place. Others are coaches or consultants who want to scale their businesses. These goals matter, but they're not what I'm referring to when I ask about your *why*.

Your *why* needs to be meaningful to you *and* your future members. In fact, a powerful *why* will resonate with your future members as much as it does with you. It will likely connect to an obstacle you've overcome in your personal or professional life which you yearn to help others solve as well. In a *Forbes* article about why communities matter, writer Tracy Brower says:

"Strong communities have a significant sense of purpose. People's roles have meaning in the bigger picture of the community, and each group member understands how their work connects to others and adds value to the whole. As community members, people don't just want to lay bricks; they want to build a cathedral."

As my clients and I have come to discover, a community concept is much more than who you bring together; it comes down to what problem your community aims to solve.

One of my community-building friends introduced me to Ayelet Baron, recognized as one of *Forbes'* top global female futurists and an inspirational community builder. Ayelet brings together amazing people in her Conscious Community who are pioneering healthy paths, asking questions, and connecting in new ways. In my interview with Ayelet for *The Community Strategy Podcast*, she shared her insights on finding a purpose.

From "Episode 55: Find Calm creating a purposeful community with Ayelet Baron":

 "What if we followed our heart? What if we got our minds aligned with our hearts? What I find in conversations is that many of us feel alone and isolated. The three biggest currencies of where we're headed are our trust in relationships, community, and the world."

This statement reflects the values and purpose she brings to the communities she runs: to create a world where we approach life differently.

When Ayelet left Cisco after fifteen years, she continued to speak at her audience's behest. The companies she speaks to are some of the biggest in the world, and they desperately need her message of humanity. She went on to say, "If you don't understand why you're building the community and somebody is telling you that that's what you must do to be successful, you've got to sit down and say, is that true for me, and what does community mean?"

Provide a Specific Solution for a Specific Audience

When I first started my community, I yearned to provide a space for people to find resources and calm. However, by the end of my first year, I was exhausted. I'd provided plenty of content and experiences but had struggled to gain traction. Now I know why. I hadn't clearly identified who the community was for. A wide variety of topics meant I was trying to serve everyone under the sun.

Yes, I had a compelling goal—to offer relief from anxiety and stress—but as I see now, my theme was way too large. My "finding calm" umbrella was compelling enough to attract people, but it hadn't provided a *specific* solution for a *specific* audience.

I'd recruited amazing people to speak, and I valued every single session. However, as it turned out, I'd promoted their services, offers, and products, while having no profit to show for my own goals. In my attempt to provide a calm space for others, I'd worn myself out.

As entrepreneurs know, success comes from setbacks—assuming we're willing to learn from them. In my case, the bright spot came from the members themselves. After connecting with these individuals each week from June through December, I noticed a portion of them had something in common—they were community builders themselves. They were leaders who shared my belief that people come first. They had similar goals and challenges, and I sensed I could help them. Not only did I know I could help them, but they also told me so, point blank! Over time, they told me exactly what they wanted, which allowed me to reshape my community. Listening to their needs, I launched anew. This time, the community was just for them, and it addressed their biggest pain point—isolation—by including structured cohorts.

Know Your Strengths

Listening to your people is critical when launching a community. Equally important is knowing what matters to you. If you struggle to find your own *why*, you'll have a tough time attracting the right people for any space you create. When was the last time you checked in with your strengths, values, and preferred skills (that is, skills you enjoy instead of ones you've learned but don't enjoy)?

As you explore the best direction for your business, you'll benefit from revisiting your strengths. I highly recommend taking the Clifton StrengthsFinder Top 5 Strengths assessment to identify what drives you. After taking the assessment, if you need help finding your values and preferred skills, you may want to check out YouMap® assessments, which I found helpful for developing my business.

My clients have discovered that running a community can be rewarding and profitable, but there's no getting around the fact that building and maintaining it takes energy. The better you know yourself (and your team), the better prepared you'll be to build a structure that lasts and doesn't deplete you of your resources in the process.

For this reason, I've become a certified YouMap® coach. I use these tools to help new business owners clarify their strengths, values, and preferred skills. It's also important to identify your burnout skills or skills you don't enjoy doing.

Many of my clients refer to writing, editing, or recording videos as a few of their burnout skills. For example, I may know how to edit photos, but I do not *enjoy* editing photos. I took a video editing course in college but do not enjoy editing videos, so it is a burnout skill for me. This means it would be better for me to focus on skills that light me up, such as writing, a skill I am good at and enjoy doing. I also continue to practice and improve this skill.

If I needed a video edited and had the budget to hire someone, that is exactly what I would do, so I can focus on the work I love, which is spending time with clients and writing. Some might see these merely as tasks, but I have a background and training in visual arts and journalism, so I'm skilled in these areas and have identified them as the type of work I enjoy doing.

I've seen a lot of new community builders become stuck thinking they need everything to be perfect in the beginning, and that's unrealistic. You don't need a website right away, a perfect logo, or a ton of podcast episodes. You can start without those things. Focus on the core aspects of what it is you want to do and let go of the rest.

Knowing what you want to do and what you don't want to do will help you identify your signature programs or community concept, that is if you still haven't clarified who you will bring together and what problem you will help them solve.

Some clients become stuck in this phase for a long time because they can't figure out how they can offer an experience that is different from anything which currently exists in the marketplace.

This framework (which 1 learned from Mighty Networks) has helped me, and it is something 1 use with clients every day. "1 bring together (ideal members) who (problem they have) to (what they'll do together to solve this problem) so they can (an outcome they desire and want to do with others)."

Chapter Snapshot

☆ Although there are more ways than ever to connect digitally with others, users of online platforms have reported feeling they are not participating in meaningful conversations or they do not have a voice.

☆ Online communities are needed now more than ever, and building communities has three important elements: a place to meet digitally to be seen, heard, and valued; a routine, habit, or ritual members do together; and a common challenge, goal, desire, or need.

☆ Successful communities solve a specific problem for a specific audience.

☆ Building and running a community takes energy. When planning your community, know your strengths (and your team's strengths).

Action Items

1. If you're considering launching a community, make a list on one side of the page of what energizes you about the idea. On the other side, list your doubts.
2. If you already run a community, write what you enjoy on one side of the page. On the other side, write what burns you out. What have you learned?
3. This week, share your thoughts from this section with one person. Contact a friend, colleague, or team member to discuss your thoughts.

Questions to Consider

Why do you want to lead an online community?

Think of your members. Why do they want to be a part of your community?

What specific problem will your community solve? How?

How passionate are you about this and why?

Glen Onoko Falls, Lehigh River, Eastern Pennsylvania

"Clear is kind. Unclear is unkind."

— *Brené Brown*

CHAPTER 2

Develop Your Community Strategy

One summer, I spent hours as a river rafting guide, kayaking the Lehigh River in the Poconos of Pennsylvania. The water was usually murky; if I dropped something in the river, it was lost. The same applies to any community; without clarity, you risk losing it.

A community cannot successfully launch without strategic preparation, strong leadership, and a clear goal. Understanding the roles and responsibilities of community leaders, hosts, and managers is important.

To build a community strategy, there are five stages I take my clients through to develop what will become the foundation of their roadmap for success.

- ☆ Stage 1, Community Concept: What's the *why* behind your community idea?
- ☆ Stage 2, Community Curiosity: Who is this community for, and what's in it for them?

☆ Stage 3, Community Clarity: How will this community transform or support its members?

☆ Stage 4, Community Structure: What content, events, and programs will support members?

☆ Stage 5, Community Strategy Launch Plan: When, why, where, how, and by whom will this community be shared with my audience?

Determining your community strategy (and your launch or relaunch plan) will require going through the stages outlined above. Existing business owners will want to determine how a community fits within the organization and how it aligns with their existing business goals. For new community builders, you'll need to determine how the community will fit in with your existing commitments, jobs, and responsibilities.

This book focuses on individuals who want to launch (or relaunch) an online community, course, or program as a paid offer to begin or grow a business. Determining your community goals means aligning your community's mission with your future plans for the business.

A business that offers products or services benefits from an online community as it allows that business to connect and build deeper relationships with its customers, clients, and audience.

An individual who wants to start a coaching program, create a certification for new industry experts, or lead online workshops and networking events needs to find a way to support the venture with revenue from an existing business, through funding from investors, or by bootstrapping.

If you aren't familiar with the term "bootstrapping," it refers to individuals who don't have capital to launch a startup and need to fund it themselves, a concept that includes most of the individuals I've discovered in the community-building world. So, unless you are independently wealthy, you'll need to find a way to cover the cost of running your own community, which can be very expensive.

Most clients I work with want to quit working for others and launch a program, course, or community that gives them not only income, but also time back into their lives. The unfortunate truth is that many people mistake building a community for launching a self-study course, which is a totally different experience.

To clarify the difference between a community concept that is passive versus one that is focused on sharing wisdom is the building of ecosystems, outlined in the examples in the coming paragraphs.

A self-study course I buy and complete alone by watching videos, filling out worksheets, and asking questions within a private group is not a community. Not only will people struggle to finish the course without support (most people need a nudge), but they are also less likely to ask a question for fear of being seen by their peers as stupid. This leads to little-to-no engagement because so many of the course participants don't feel supported and are afraid to ask questions. Members will fall off and will refrain from taking action. If they do manage to finish the course, they may not truly implement the teachings into their life.

Now imagine a twelve-week learning cohort focused on gaining clarity on your community concept with the support of peers, actionable steps, and activities that connect members. This is a community focused on encouraging members to share what they've learned in a natural way with no teacher, but rather a guide who can share personal experiences.

In the second example, you are able to share your ideas, challenges, and needs directly with your peers in various ways that work for your schedule and your preferences for communication. The host of this cohort listens to your questions and provides updated resources or materials when gaps in the program are discovered by members.

Cocreating with your members not only helps you because you don't have to have everything figured out at the beginning, but it also invites your members to be a part of the community-building process. However, this will take longer, and for that reason, you need to decide how you will financially support the efforts of the program.

I Launch My First Version of Find Calm Here

When I first launched the Find Calm Here community, it was a wellness initiative to help people in my hometown find calm in their daily lives. My *why* had come to me over five years of coping with intense stress and anxiety in my personal development journey. Through healthy and holistic practices, I'd found ways to avoid self-sabotage and overindulgence.

Driven to leave a corporate job that drained me, I yearned to strike out on my own. I wondered whether I could help myself while also helping others find their own freedom from depression. The concept led me to recruit speakers, schedule workshops, and develop a coaching program for those seeking to live their ideal lives. In time, the program became a virtual community that served a network of facilitators, community builders, practitioners, and friends, featuring collaborative sessions and interactive coaching.

My Monetary Strategy Fails

Although the community was active in some ways, it failed to generate income. Despite doing everything online experts say is needed for a successful launch, I didn't have enough validation for the community's purpose. I discovered, to my surprise and frustration, my audience wasn't willing to pay for a monthly membership. Unwilling to give up, I opened the community for free and spent the next six months evaluating the best way to relaunch with a new business model. This involved conducting discovery interviews, speaking with fellow community builders, and developing new ideas.

My Members Provide Clarity for a New Concept

When my fellow community builders approached me about consulting and design services, I was inspired to develop a new business model. Needing to recoup the money I'd already invested, I focused on recruiting clients through referrals. I set up a rate structure that would allow me to build the community my people were asking for. I spent time building people's trust within the community and gained clarity on my new concept.

I Craft a New Business Model

By this time, I'd discovered the difficulty of building a membership model without an established audience. I decided to try a program structure with a fixed group, timeline, and outcomes. That fall, I began building my consulting business while still running wellness events inside the Find Calm Here community. I'd had a positive experience with a mastermind group from the online community of which I was a member and felt it was a great structure to try for my first beta program, so I reached out to several friends who had expressed interest in starting an online business.

Working with five new entrepreneurs, I developed a ninety-day mastermind group for business development. I ran it for the first time, and, unlike my first model, I found success. Feedback from participants was so positive that I offered another one soon after, that time a ninety-day mastermind group exclusively meant for community builders.

The program included biweekly virtual gatherings, interactive workshops, worksheets, resources, and sessions for participants to share their community strategies and gain feedback. At the end, I sent out a survey to gain insight into what worked and what could be improved.

I Reopen Find Calm Here

At the conclusion of the second mastermind group, I announced my relaunch plan for the Find Calm Here community, which I'd be serving exclusively to community builders.

The first phase included informing existing members that the community was transitioning to a paid space and offering them a discounted two-month trial to experience the new structure.

The second phase involved reaching out to a variety of prospects, including past clients and people I'd spoken to but had never worked with. I posted an announcement on the *Find Calm Here* blog and promoted it on my podcast. Formerly called *Find Calm Here,* it became *The Community Strategy Podcast.*

The third phase included a slow launch with sessions to get to know the new members and refine how I could help them. They asked for step-by-step guides for community-building tasks, so I created blueprints for launching, onboarding, and member growth. However, I discovered that members were still less engaged than I had expected.

I realized I was still putting the focus on myself and not on them. The group sessions were designed as "office hours" that allowed them to ask me questions and gain support, but this format didn't encourage them to offer encouragement, support, or solutions to one another.

Then I asked our members what they'd like to do together, and they suggested a book club. Together, we successfully created a community-led book club, which took the focus off me as host and empowered the community members to lead, connect, and collaborate.

As this example shows, I had an idea, ran with it, and listened to my members' needs. I discovered what worked best for them as members and for me as the host. Even more, I relaunched the community with the understanding that my strategy would evolve as I continued to ask questions.

During Episode 90 of *The Community Strategy Podcast*, I asked my guest, Laurence McCahill, if he had had a community strategy before launching The Happy Startup School, a home for purpose-driven entrepreneurs and leaders who want to make money, do good, and be happy. He said faith had validated the concept from other projects he'd done. These were in-person meetups that he developed over time. He now hosts them as a summer camp and has found great success. As a member of this community, I can tell you there are many amazing humans involved.

Laurence also highlighted the importance of a partner or collaborator to bounce community-building ideas off of and to help gain insights. His business partner, Carlos Saba, brings a different energy and enthusiasm and the ability to ask critical questions. Their collaboration allows for a community strategy that supports everyone's vision, mission, and goals.

If you don't have a collaborator or a partner, find one! If that sounds challenging, consider starting with a consultant who can provide an outsider's perspective. Search for someone who can walk you through a discovery process that actively supports the needs of your organization, business, or program.

Regardless of how you approach your strategy, I recommend following the four community-building elements I've developed for my own clients. This structured approach helps to keep you focused on a specific outcome or transformation you can promote to your members.

I call it the CALM Method, and *any community builder can benefit from moving through it thoughtfully.*

CALM METHOD™ FOR COMMUNITY DESIGN
* ☆ Clarity on your unique concept.
* ☆ Awareness of your validation sources.
* ☆ Learning about what structure works best for you.
* ☆ Motion through action.

Clarity: Not only will you need to gain clarity on the community concept for yourself, but you will also need to make sure it is easy for your members to understand. Therefore, the first step is to focus on developing a clear community concept and a unique offering. This will include looking at the marketplace and finding something different to offer based on your life's work, experiences, and challenges.

Awareness: Not only will you need to confirm that your potential members understand your message and concept, but you also will need to be aware they can actually validate your idea and express interest. When you speak with your potential members to learn more about their needs, challenges, and problems, you'll begin to build a relationship with them. However, you will need to ask them what problem they have and how they've solved it in the past. If they only want to watch videos and do work on their own, a community isn't a good solution for them. Alternatively, if you become aware that your ideal members need a supportive community to help them transition during challenging life phases—parenthood, owning a business, or retirement—a community would be a viable solution for them.

Learning: Finding out what members want to do and how they want to participate is a big part of the community-building process. You will learn, from your members, what kind of structure works best for them. You might find that members of your four-week course want to continue meeting over the next six months. You might review data from your community and realize most members aren't watching your videos but are showing up on your live office hour calls. That means members are more interested in active communication with you and each other than a recorded piece of content that may or may not solve their problem. You will learn how your members want to learn, connect, and participate within your community.

Motion: After all this work, it's time to act! With the data from your clarity, awareness, and learning opportunities, you will be able to assemble your community strategy. Depending on how complex your structure will be, this step may include designing the architecture, implementing a content calendar, managing daily operations, and facilitating virtual sessions.

Even if you don't have a team now, make it your goal to gain support as soon as you can. Despite promises from platforms that building your community will be easy, sustaining a community requires commitment. Additionally, launching requires focus and consistency, especially if you are a new business owner without an established audience. Now may not be the best time to launch if you're still working on establishing your first clients, figuring out how to charge, or building initial offers.

I learned the hard way that building an online community takes resources. To help you feel supported at every stage, I'll give examples of different strategies to design your community, with or without a team.

Develop a Community Team (Even Before You Hire Them)

So many community builders either plan to do everything themselves or jump right into hiring a community manager. Instead, I recommend first gaining clarity about your strategy. Yes, having someone to help you moderate and handle mentorship is great, but if you don't know how the community will support your business model, or if you don't have a business yet, it may be too soon to know exactly what that support should look like or whether you will need any at all. Sometimes, when several people are involved, distractions increase and break the focus needed to strategize.

A client I worked with had challenges in this area. She attempted to onboard her team while still developing her strategy, which led to confusion for everyone. As the host, you will set the vision for your online community's future. You'll guide and support the members until you're ready to bring in the right support for your community.

You may hire professionals who offer services to support you as the host or who engage team members to manage aspects of the design, community building, content writing, copywriting, marketing materials, education, or funding. We will talk about this more in the upcoming sections. I hope you can see how much goes into creating a community with purpose, but it's worth the work if you are dedicated to the process.

When starting the search to fill your community roles, you may find different definitions than I offer here. Be aware, there are many different types of communities and infinite possibilities for a community's structure and strategy. The more complex a community strategy is, the more time it will take to educate your team and audience.

Strategy 1: Run It by Yourself

A community host sets the vision, mission, and purpose of an online community. This person makes decisions about the community structure and develops the community strategy (and launch plan) through the phases of the CALM Method.™

A single-host structure comes with limitations on time and resources. It is completely dependent on your ability to keep yourself accountable throughout the community-building journey. Without a community program facilitator, you will be the person guiding members during virtual meetups and onboarding new people into the community.

You will also be the person who will market and promote your community on social media, through emails, or with live streaming. If you intend to build a community on your own, consider how to keep these tasks minimal or eliminate what is not imperative to your program's success.

An effective way to do this is to start with a timed program, such as ninety days. This will give participants a start and end date to commit to, which will help you set expectations from the beginning.

Another benefit of a timed program is that you can create urgency. A start date requires participants to decide—either the program fits their schedule or not. They will also know when it ends, so they won't be locked into any specific "what's next" concept. You can develop your program, test it, and evaluate the results. What worked, and what didn't? From there, you will be able to decide if you want to do it again.

Another critical factor is your gathering place. Don't underestimate the importance of your chosen platform, as it will affect your participants' experience and your own. The technology available to build a community is where many of my clients become stuck.

Knowing how you'll use the platform is critical. For example, will your members connect between sessions? If you're unsure, I suggest interviewing potential members about how they want to gather.

When I hosted my initial business development mastermind group, we met weekly via Zoom. Members enjoyed it and consistently showed up. I can't say the same about the community space I'd put in place. I'd invested in a tool that allowed members to share, connect, and collaborate between our calls, but they never used it. The feedback I received was they didn't feel it was necessary because they communicated via email. This taught me about the members of my program and their lack of need for additional tools that cost me time and money to set up. Moving forward, I learned a community can look like a lot of things, and it really is up to you and your members to define what is ideal for your community culture.

Here is an example of a few community roles for a paid online community, network, or program:

1. Community Host: to guide the vision, mission, and purpose
2. Community Facilitator: to support the programming, events, or workshops
3. Community Manager: to onboard and support members and encourage participation within the community
4. Strategy Consultant: to create processes and tools to increase conversions from your marketing and advertising efforts to your programs
5. Marketing Manager: to help promote, advertise, and scale your business

Strategy 2: Run It With Help From One Team Member

When developing your strategy with a partner, it's up to you whether one or both of you will function as the community host as I've defined above, the person who will set the community structure and strategy. When working with one or more collaborators, it is best to first identify how each person will best contribute.

When launching a community as a startup with two or three people, to identify each person's strengths is to identify their role within the community. As I've outlined above, there are a few core roles a community should have when launching a paid program.

Going forward, I'll refer to the host as the person who aligns the community strategy with the business goals. Assuming you're the business owner, this will likely be you. The community facilitator is the one responsible for the community content, programming, and events.

There are a variety of ways for a community facilitator to engage, so think about what makes sense for your people, as well as each of your personalities. Make sure to clearly define who does what and how active each of you will be in taking the lead role. For example, you may decide the facilitator should be the go-between for the host and the members in lieu of a community manager (if you don't have one).

Community facilitators could be course instructors, cohosts, coaches, or advocates. For an active, forward-facing role like this, the facilitator should possess qualities such as self-awareness, eagerness to learn and adapt, empathy, integrity, dedication, service, the ability to inspire others, motivation, and strong communication skills.

A host also may bring in a community manager to help facilitate, in addition to managing the daily operations. In this case, their role may be less visible, yet it will still be vitally important to the community's health.

Community strategy, marketing, and sales support can be outsourced by hiring professional consultants or agencies to help create content, develop a launch plan, and implement a sales strategy.

One of the tasks you might ask of your community facilitator or manager includes writing a community playbook or operations manual, so new team members can be easily trained.

Additionally, community facilitators or managers may be assigned to write onboarding materials such as welcome videos, guidelines, or how-to manuals.

Strategy 3: Run It With Volunteers From Your Community

When hiring a community manager, I recommend starting within your community. Not only do these people already know the ropes, but they also tend to bring an infectious enthusiasm. The host may or may not be able to pay for this part-time role, but it's not unusual for online community managers to volunteer for reasons other than money.

Depending on the size, scale, and purpose of your community, the manager may also be responsible for content planning, event facilitation, leadership development, marketing and promotion, member onboarding, or dealing with ongoing challenges the community faces.

Designating and communicating clear responsibilities for your host, leader, and manager is key to crafting a successful strategy. Not only should you identify who will take ownership of each step, but you should also establish a timeline for the community launch or relaunch with benchmarks, goals, and outcomes.

Chapter Snapshot

☆ Launching an online community takes resources—
time, energy, and money. It also requires thought and
organization.

☆ A successful community requires a strategy behind the
concept that supports the business needs, goals, and
outcomes.

☆ The five stages of community building include concept,
curiosity, clarity, structure, and strategy.

☆ Who will run the community is up to you. Options
include running it by yourself (host only), with one other
person (host and leader), or with a team (host, leader, and
manager).

☆ Designating who does what is key to successful
community.

Action Items

Define Your Community Strategy:

1. Write out your community's purpose statement.
2. Outline a possible community structure.
3. Decide how you'll seek validation, and reach out to ideal members to gauge interest.
4. If you don't want to run it on your own, search for a community leader or manager.
5. Research potential platforms for your community and compare features with what your audience wants.

Questions to Consider

Who do you want to bring together and why?

Will your initial program start and end on designated dates?

When does it make sense to launch your community?

Who is on your team?

How will you gain supporters?

Peña de Bernal, Mexico

"*People will forget what you said, people will forget what you did, but people will never forget how you made them feel.*"

— *Maya Angelou*

CHAPTER 3

Explore Your Community Design and Structure

Standing near the top of Peña de Bernal in Central Mexico, a friend offered to take my photograph. Several of us from the Location Indie community had hiked up the formation, and I couldn't wait to come back down and enjoy drinking from a real coconut, something one of our hosts, Jason, had described in great detail. His story had my mouth watering just thinking about it!

The memorable hike, refreshing coconut drink, and meal afterward are the kinds of experiences you remember for a lifetime. We talked about life, posed for photos, ate, laughed, and enjoyed walking around town. One of the attendees flew a drone high above all of us to take a nice group photo. The day was spent with friends connecting, building relationships, and enjoying good views and food. This experience describes the way most communities have flourished for thousands of years.

I'm sharing this story to emphasize the importance of creating memorable experiences for your members. *That's* what matters to them. When we focus too much on technology, our outcomes as a host, or our own financial needs, we diminish the potential of having amazing connections with our members.

Most new community builders become stuck trying to establish their online structure. They become caught up in finding the best way or the right way, instead of simply starting. It is important to focus not on the technology, but on the people, so start with them. Most of my clients skip that step. Then they launch quickly without the validation of their community concept, only to wonder why their community hasn't gained new members or retained existing ones.

Often, it's at this point new community builders find me. In this chapter, I'll outline examples of community structures that have worked successfully for my clients. As you read, remember there's no *one* right way. Even if something has worked well for others, it may not work that way for you.

As you read, consider what matters to you and your people. Your community should reflect the learning styles, connections, and social activities you desire. Think about what experiences you're willing to try. Not everything has to be the right fit, and sometimes you won't know until you get your hands dirty.

LET'S TALK ABOUT THE FIVE ELEMENTS OF COMMUNITY DESIGN

1. Architecture: a strategy for the layout of a community
2. Member Content: written, visual, audio, and video content organized for the community
3. Experience: onboarding, communication, notifications, and interactions
4. Culture: the tone, guidelines, and expectations of your community
5. Participation: methods for members to share, connect, and communicate within the community

Architecture

The architecture of an online community refers to the structure you build. This includes the features, member benefits, user experience, and structuring of content and resources within the online space. A well-thought-out community aligns with the vision, mission, and purpose established by the group's host. Leading an online community requires deciding how you want to communicate with your members and understanding how they enjoy connecting with each other.

When working with a client to restructure their community, I start by identifying a purpose for each area of the community. For example, one client had a podcast and shared weekly episodes through a podcast supporter area within the community. In addition, there was an area for members to connect with each other where events were posted, but the members didn't seem to be engaging there. Instead, they only participated in the podcast supporter space, so this is what we decided to change.

Note that the words area and space can be used interchangeably to describe the destination to which you are sending your members to participate and engage. As with driving, you set your GPS for one destination—not twelve—unless you are on a road trip and planning to stop at a lot of places along the way. If that's the case, take photos for me!

The point is you need to make sure you point your members to the right destination and that they understand why that is a space where they want to spend time (virtually or in person).

A common problem for many community builders is knowing how many destinations to have available for people to meet, connect, and engage. When this particular client and I focused on solving the key challenge—lack of member engagement—we realized members didn't have permission to share posts within the community, which is why they were posting in a different space! In addition, the members didn't know where to post because there were so many areas, which, as one member said in a discovery interview, was confusing. We learned to dedicate one core area for members to engage, which helped to focus energy, instead of splitting it between different areas.

The structure you establish will influence other design elements such as your community's culture. It will provide the framework for your host, leader, or manager to help your people build habits and cultivate rituals. Think about how you want to communicate; your personal communication style is an important factor to consider. In addition, your community must be easy to access.

When envisioning your structure, research communities you're attracted to as a potential member. An activity I recommend for this stage is to visit an online community you haven't been to for a while. Log in as if it's the first time. Pay attention to everything you experience. What's the navigation like? What features do you see? How easy is it to find resources? Is there a chat space? Who posts what? What are the guidelines? Can you ask questions? Is there a member directory? Where do you go for help?

In addition to scoping out the group with fresh eyes, check out fellow community members. Introduce yourself to one member and see if they respond. Ask a question of the host(s) and see how they reply. Do they reply to you with comments or questions? Take notes on what it is about the design that you love and what you don't love. Notice if there is too much text or too many complex explanations. Ideally, everything should be clear and easy to understand.

Evaluate your time spent in this community. Think about the value of investing your energy and money there. Consider the other members and identify whether they're people you want to know better. These things will help you design the architecture of your own community. Being thoughtful early on will create confidence in your decisions once you're up and running.

The last thing I'll ask you to do is to figure out if you'd like to build your community on or off social media. Define your answers in writing, outlining why it is important to host this community on a specific platform (if that's the case).

You'll need to determine if you've got what it takes to learn a platform or if you'll hire a designer. I strongly recommend hiring someone for technology support. Remember to be crystal clear on your community's concept before spending too much time, effort, and money on any platform.

Content

Another common challenge for new community builders is excessive content. It's easy to become caught up thinking you need to spend hours building content, but this is rarely why your people are there.

One client hired me to help her build an online course and community. She was still in the process of creating the course content, and it eventually became held up and prevented her from launching. She was so focused on finishing the videos that she didn't focus on the people who would be watching them. When it came time to answer challenging questions about her offer (who the course was for and what problem it would solve), she couldn't provide clear, concise responses.

Another client hired me to conduct ideal member interviews during which one of the members bluntly stated she'd be willing to pay for engagement but not content. Because there was already a massive amount online, she'd rather invest in connection. Her motivation was meeting like-minded folks from around the world, people she couldn't have met otherwise. When laying your own foundation, never forget that people seek out an online community to find those who have similar interests and values in a way they wouldn't find anywhere else.

Simply speaking, online community members are looking for a dedicated place to share challenges, thoughts, or ideas. They want to ask questions, respond in support of other members, and feel their ideas are valued.

Social media is no longer a "warm and fuzzy" place to connect with friends or followers. Too often, people share opinions without considering the consequences, and when they use pseudonyms, they're likely to stoke animosity.

There are some individuals who don't want to hide behind fake profiles and want to build real relationships or improve existing ones. It takes courage to be vulnerable on social media when life isn't going well, so struggling and needing support isn't something most people are likely to post online.

If you are like me, you tend to retreat into your house and stay there, feeling very disconnected from society. Everyone is busy, and everyone has problems. How do we manage the stresses of life if we have no one to talk to about them? What do we do if there's simply no one to offer support when we don't know how to heal from a breakup or a job loss? Where do we go? Individuals are left to seek out relationships online, but they have no idea if the person on the other end is real or trustworthy.

From a business perspective, the difference between social media and online communities is that social media is more focused on views and advertising. The goal for all content on social media is to increase the number of views, and that is how the algorithms are set up for businesses to make money. That means you, as a creator, must "pay to play" the game on social media by purchasing advertising to be seen by your own fans, audience, or customers.

As the host or leader, consider the kind of sharing your platform will allow. How do you want your members to express themselves? Will they contribute documents, images, GIFs, videos? Will they use apps to send and receive messages? Everyone has their own way of communicating, and it is increasingly challenging to serve all people in all forms of communication (text, video, audio, visual, experiential, informal, formal, and professional or casual).

Deciding to launch an online community on a platform doesn't solve all your problems. The questions above will influence your choice of platform but remember to prioritize connection over complicated technology.

As we've established, the mission of your community drives everything, and your content is no exception. Suppose your purpose is to facilitate deep, meaningful conversations through regular virtual calls. In that case, there may be less activity between calls on a feed or forum because the engagement happens during that live session. If you're hosting a course or facilitating group coaching, you may need to provide a space for sharing experiences and challenges between sessions. You'll need to decide what additional kind of interaction, if any, is needed to support your members' experiences.

As a community leader, one of your key jobs is creating a safe space. As you plan, be thoughtful about the number of members you're gathering at a given time. Breakout rooms are an effective tool for helping members feel heard. Let's say you'll be giving a discussion prompt during your live call. If you have more than five participants, consider breaking them into pairs or small groups.

For groups of five to ten attendees, consider putting them into pairs. Forming smaller, more intimate discussion groups will allow them to build relationships with one person at a time. If there's an odd number of people, you can be a partner as well. For larger groups of twenty or more, I'd suggest putting them into groups of four or five people and asking them to identify a group leader who will take notes and report to the larger group when everyone returns.

You should also think about how your members will want to connect between calls. Would they feel more inclined to share thoughts, ideas, or challenges with a smaller private group? If so, think about how to organize these groups. Would they rather text with another member directly? In that case, would they use a chat feature, or would they potentially prefer to post or comment on a group activity feed? Some members would rather talk via voice messaging software or applications such as Voxer and WhatsApp.

Experience

As a community host, leader, or manager, it's your job to facilitate your members' experience. Don't expect them to jump in on their own; you need to show them what to do and how to do it. Onboarding is the first experience your members will have with the community, so you will want to ensure they aren't left with more questions than answers.

It is traditional to start an onboarding process by inviting new members to join via email and encouraging them to introduce themselves and read the rules of the group. This is something you've likely seen in Facebook groups.

The problem with this is that it isn't how we experience onboarding in real life. When you join a new in-person community, before introducing yourself, you likely learn what the community is about, who attends meetings, and why it's important to participate.

Start with the purpose of your community, and let members know why you've invited them to take this journey with you. Guide them through how to experience the community and how to make the most out of their time there.

On your own or with your team, think about drafting a roadmap for members' journey, from where they start to where you want them to end up. Then, for any stage of the journey that's relevant to your community, lay out how you will support them along the way. As you do this, it's also important to be upfront about what your space can't or won't do. If it provides support for people struggling with anxiety, but you aren't a trained mental health professional, then say so. Make sure members know if they have specific issues, this may not be the right place to discuss those health challenges.

Maybe you are a coach and want to help others feel healthier and happier. Finding the right home for your coaching materials, videos, and documentation is critical, so members adopt the content and don't become stuck on the unfamiliar technology. Many people choose to create a Facebook group, for example, because many Gen Xers and millennials are familiar with that platform, so there are fewer potential barriers to your content and resources.

There are many challenges with social media, and as I've discussed, you don't own your content, so choose software that you purchase. Popular course platform software includes Teachable, Kajabi, Thinkific, Maven, or Podia. If you are only interested in hosting a self-study course with no member-to-member connection, these platforms might be a good fit for you. While these solutions are great for teaching individuals, they don't help us implement what we learn. The community component really makes a difference in putting ideas into practice.

Robyn Conley Downs found this out the hard way after trying to add a community component to her course platform and discovering it was not the seamless experience she wanted to offer her members. She sought out a cohesive platform that offered members both step-by-step guides and a place to connect with one another.

Robyn reached out to me after listening to an episode of my podcast because she learned about Mighty Networks and wanted to combine her content and community on the platform. She had worked with clients in her coaching practice and has since designed a certification program based on her proven methods.

The experience for members in her online community differs depending on where they are in their wellness journeys. Since Robyn has a wide audience, members might join for a variety of reasons.

Robyn has several offerings, so any potential member could benefit depending on their needs.

Here's an example of a member journey for someone just starting their journey:

1. A potential member, I'll call her Deb, visits Robyn's website.
2. Deb enjoys the content and continues to visit over the next few months.

3. Deb signs up for Robyn's email newsletter to receive updates.
4. Robyn's new subscriber opens her emails and reads them when she has time.
5. A few months pass, until Robyn announces a new community, The Feel Good Society, for the launch of her book, *The Feel Good Effect.*
6. Deb decides to sign up for a paid twelve-week book study group which includes group coaching.
7. Deb joins the group, and she's welcomed by members. She gets to know a few members during the weekly meetups over the twelve weeks, and starts to build relationships and make healthy changes in her life.
8. By the time the course ends, Deb is eager to participate in Robyn's next offering!

This is just one member journey, but someone who's more advanced and wants to build a wellness business might choose to work with Robyn to become a certified coach. Robyn's community can serve both beginners and advanced level individuals.

The journey for someone who's advanced might look like this:

1. Sue has been through her own wellness journey and wants to help others while also building a coaching business.
2. Sue starts to look for programs for health or wellness coaches online and talks with friends and colleagues to figure out how to start her business.
3. Sue discovers Robyn's coaching program and really identifies with the message.
4. She subscribes to Robyn's email newsletter or purchases her book. Over time, Sue becomes an avid fan of Robyn's teachings and practices.

5. One of Robyn's emails states she's launching a new coaching certification only for her past clients who she will personally train. Sue eagerly fills out the application to receive more information about the program and receives an invitation to schedule a call with Robyn.

6. When Robyn and Sue meet virtually, they are instantly a good fit. Sue shares with Robyn that she's read *The Feel Good Effect* and wants to become a wellness coach. Robyn tells Sue about her six-month paid program, which provides individual and group support to make sure she has everything she needs to launch a successful coaching business.

7. Sue is excited to learn from her favorite coach and finally launch the business she has been dreaming of for years. She gets to meet other coaches, learn what is working for them, and utilize their support as she launches her business. It's a win for all!

As you probably discovered when investigating communities you've liked, there are many ways to provide an experience. Experiences can be ongoing or timed, short or long. Deciding on the frequency, level of content, and time commitment will help you identify the best structure for your community with your current resources.

Maybe you dream of launching an eight-week program. Are you ready to facilitate that right now? If not, be honest with yourself and your team. Just because you don't have time now, doesn't mean it won't happen, but you certainly don't want to overcommit and end up unable to deliver.

As you prepare, make a list of the most important action steps needed to meet your goals. Prioritize those from most important to least important. Once your priorities are clear, you'll see the best structure for your community based on your needs, lifestyle, goals, and vision.

Culture

Community culture can be explained as how you invite members to participate, share, connect, and learn together. It is the path for members to feel seen, valued, and heard. Culture is written into your community guidelines, demonstrated in your member testimonials, and expressed by members when they talk about your community to others.

Culture inside a community is understood as the language used, sometimes referred to as jargon, that only the members of that community would understand. A community culture could include the way members interact (in person, on a video call, through text) and the depths to which relationships are forged.

Creating a community culture doesn't simply happen; you need to actively nurture it. I've already shared the common pitfall, which is overly complex technology, but please allow me to repeat it once more: Don't let platform selection hold up your entire launch!

The onboarding process will be an important part of your community's culture as well as your members' experience of it. A combination of elements working together can help members have a great experience and build a community structure that sets the foundation for success.

There are many ways people can engage with your community, so let yourself have some fun as you brainstorm how their participation will align with your strategy and concept.

Start by gaining clarity. Make a list of questions and reach out to your ideal members for feedback. Ask about the features, functionality, and experience they'd derive the most benefit from. Don't forget to also consider the experience you want to have as host.

From "Episode 86: Leading a Global Mindfulness Community with Elisha Goldstein":

 "We've tried many things, from volunteer-led to donation to free community structures, and we've found that sometimes the technology can create friction. How we've overcome these challenges was to keep it simplistic; we made it easy for everyone."

Elisha Goldstein, host of The Mindful Living Collective, hired me to restructure his online community. My first step was determining what he, as the host, wanted to change about the existing structure. Next, I evaluated its engagement, organization, and navigation. I then provided him with my recommendations to streamline the experience. To clean up his space, we removed content his members weren't using.

Over the course of a few weeks, I worked with him to learn more about his members. We sent out a short survey through email and within the community's platform, and what we received back were valuable insights about their experiences. They shared why they spend time in the community and the impact it has had on their lives. They described how fellow members have helped them navigate challenges in their lives and what they'd like to see going forward.

Before we sent the survey, we knew members wanted daily live meditations led by trained facilitators. However, by asking directly, we found out things we didn't know, such as when to host these meditations or for how long.

Thanks to the survey, we confirmed that the community was full of people who had similar challenges and wished to practice mindfulness together. They also explained what allowed them to feel safe and seen.

When asked, "What do you want from an online mindfulness community?" many members shared the following:

* To connect directly with like-minded people striving to live mindfully.
* To have a nonjudgmental and supportive space to share experiences.
* To learn more about myself through reflection, interaction with others, and professional guidance.

Hearing his members express what they valued renewed my client's confidence in the culture he'd built and illuminated new features to support his members.

From that experience, we focused on making sure to provide space for the members to connect more intentionally during the coaching sessions. In addition, we highlighted the accountability program, which he calls the Accountabuddy program.

The biggest step in understanding your community culture is talking with your ideal members, whether through conversations or a written survey. Let them tell you how they want to show up. As you prepare, think back to the communities where you've felt seen and valued, which might make it easier to gather this feedback.

In his book, *Tribes: We Need You to Lead Us*, Seth Godin shares his vision of rallying followers, employees, investors, customers, clients, readers, or fans around an idea:

1. Leaders create a culture around their goal and involve others in that culture.
2. Leaders have an extraordinary curiosity about the world they're trying to change. Leaders use charisma (in a variety of forms) to attract and motivate followers.
3. Leaders communicate their vision of the future.
4. Leaders commit to a vision and make decisions based on that commitment.
5. Leaders connect their followers to one another.

Participation

Once you have envisioned the community architecture, content, experience, and culture, you can jump into what the members will actually be doing. If you haven't yet considered where your ideal members are on their journey, now is a good time to do so.

Are they at the beginning of a journey, or are they in transition? What decisions do they need to make? Suppose the community is for people who are building their first businesses. In that case, they will need significant resources, support, and guidance. If you serve founders of thriving businesses, your focus will be different. These individuals may be too busy for content and instead may want professional networking or peer support. Depending on their goals, your members may participate through live calls, interactive workshops, or an online forum.

It's not uncommon for new communities to be focused on content developed by the host. Still, I encourage you to consider a different perspective. What if your main driving force was the people who show up and participate? I'm not saying you shouldn't provide resources and tools, but you may be surprised how little time your people will spend on them. Shifting into this model can take time. In my experience with established communities, it can take two or three years to transition a space into one where the members, not the host or leader, create the content.

Not everyone wants to create a course, lead a coaching program, or start a networking group. Some people want to share their favorite kinds of content, specifically music.

One of my favorite things to do is go to local pubs and enjoy live music. Over the past ten years, I've built a relationship with local musicians and venues. There was a time I considered becoming a music promoter—someone who goes around to all the venues and helps bands book shows.

When I met Benji Vaughn, the Founder of Disciple Media, a community platform for startups, non-profits, and emerging artists, I knew he'd be a great guest for *The Community Strategy Podcast*.

Disciple Media supports a wide range of musicians, influencers, creators, wellness coaches, YouTubers, politicians, and celebrity chefs, all looking for a platform that, unlike Facebook or a website, empowers community hosts.

Disciple gives members a way not only to find their audience, but also to build, manage, and control their own private social apps. The platform is trusted by over 700 customers in over twenty different industries across the globe, from Bollywood to Croatia. He's worked with the biggest musicians in the world, including The Rolling Stones and Luke Bryan.

In "Episode 97: From Music to Members," he says, "This world needs more contributions and less content consumption. If it's rewarding and giving value to people, you should be getting rewarded for creating that. In ten years' time, some of the largest businesses will be community-led."

One nonprofit I worked with wanted to launch their online community by hosting a challenge. We decided to start by involving the staff in team-building activities and sharing those experiences online. Later, we asked the staff to help invite new members by encouraging them to share their thoughts in the comments of posts and cheer them on when they had insights or valuable contributions. We rewarded the most active members of the challenge with badges such as community leader, community encourager, and community inspirational supporter.

The biggest draw to an online community is that members can receive feedback about their problems, projects, or ideas. Receiving immediate suggestions from a group of peers, in a safe space, is extremely valuable; indeed, it's worth paying for. If you have a book idea, you probably won't post that on your Facebook page or in an Instagram story. However, if you were part of a support group with new and experienced authors, you may be more inclined to share.

Within that safe space, you would feel encouraged to share your true thoughts, knowing you'd gain feedback to inspire you and clarify the concept, rather than tear it down. Contrast this experience with that of posting on social media, where someone might simply say, "Nice idea." An intentional community will foster real conversation about where to take an idea.

Your online community can be that kind of place where like-minded people receive critical feedback and meaningful support. With this format, you'll have the power to gather the right experts and peers and cultivate an environment that allows them to thrive.

Community Structures

Now that we've covered the stages of designing your community, let's talk about various ways you can structure it. As always, I'll provide some examples from clients and my own experiences.

The most important part here is not to take these examples and copy them. That's what I did initially, and it was how my first launch failed. I tried to fit my community concept, vision, strategy, and structure into a box that someone else had built, which is why it was never fully adopted. If you have been completing the worksheets and action items in this book, you'll hopefully have some clarity about your community concept.

Community building, as with entrepreneurship, is all about making decisions. It takes time to think through these decisions, and that requires you to slow down.

LET'S REVIEW A FEW DECISIONS YOU'LL NEED TO CONSIDER
- ☆ **A community concept** is what makes your space unique. You will need to decide on a specific idea—only one—that is yours, not someone else's. This was discussed in the beginning of the book as identifying your strengths and what you are known for, so you can build an audience and community around your life experiences.
- ☆ **Your ideal members** are who you want to have as a part of your community. You must decide who is a good fit for you and your offer, program, course, or membership. You should focus on one specific group of people to start, and you can expand your network once you have succeeded

with your first small community. You can't serve both beginners and advanced individuals in the same course because they are at different levels of understanding. In the earlier example of Robyn, the two groups wouldn't have launched at the same time; she decided to start with the people who had more experience and wanted to invest with her and her coaching certification.

☆ **Clarity** can be achieved once you know what makes your community unique, the problem the community solves, and your ideal members. You must decide on one problem that will be solved, one that people won't be able to resolve on their own and with which they will need support.

☆ **Community architecture**, which we've been discussing in this chapter, is the next phase, after deciding the destination, design, and structure of an online community. This includes deciding if your events or meetups will occur in person, online, or through hybrid options. It also includes deciding on the content you'll offer, how you want to experience the community as a host, and what the experience will be like for the members.

The marketing world tends to promote complex offers to provide the prospect of options. However, giving your potential members too many options will lead to them taking no action at all and never signing up. The more complex it is, the harder it will be to explain and understand. When someone doesn't immediately see how they fit within your community, you will lose them as a member before they've even joined.

HERE ARE A FEW THINGS TO CONSIDER ABOUT A COMMUNITY STRUCTURE

1. Consider your bandwidth to lead, host, develop, market, promote, and grow this program or membership.

2. New community builders should start with *one* structure and try it for a period of time to see how it fits, then decide on the next steps.

3. If you don't have a team, truly consider how each structure will work for you. If you are working a full-time job, and you are a single mother of two, you simply will not have as much time as a single individual with no children who is doing this work full-time and has a virtual assistant, a marketing team, and a hired technology support team for the community design and website management.

Starting Small: Cohorts as a Community Structure

When I launched the Find Calm Here community, I started with small cohorts to gain a sense of what common obstacles they faced to finding calm in daily life. A *cohort* refers to people who have common characteristics, and it's also a formal term to describe a small class. I hosted sessions for mindful living and minimalism, and my cohort shared their challenges with each other.

At the time, I was starting to think about creating content for the members. I put together worksheets to help them envision their ideal day and create it with their actions. The community was structured around support; the content was never intended to be the reason someone would join. Rather, it was about empowering members to build relationships with each other.

If you're building a community from scratch, I cannot come close to stressing the importance of starting small when deciding which structure will work best for you. Equally important, pay close attention to what your members want. When my audience told me how I could start supporting community builders, I pivoted.

Once I let go of the idea that I had to provide continuous education, I decided to offer a weekly support call instead, and I was amazed. I was doing less work, but the group showed up more consistently.

Before long, this group became a cohort. The same people repeatedly showed up, learning about and actively supporting each other in the process. The biggest lesson I learned was that it's a lot easier to create a cohort.

Still, it took time to work out the kinks, which made it harder to set a price. Therefore, a small beta cohort is a good place to start. If you are new to building an online community (or even if you're not), try a model that's focused on support more so than education. Below, I'll share what you need to create a cohort, as well as a few examples of different cohort structures.

WHAT YOU NEED TO CREATE A BETA COHORT

1. A desire to gather others around a topic, interest, or challenge
2. A group of three to fifteen people willing to meet consistently for a period of time, which you can define based on your understanding of the group
3. A place to gather, which can be anything from a coffee shop to a Zoom call

A Self-Study or Self-Guided Learning Course

In a self-study course, the instructor builds out training, resources, lessons, and homework, but the participants have freedom to choose how much time they want to dedicate to the course. The benefit of self-study is that participants can work within their own timeframes and at their own pace. The challenge, though, is there are no deadlines or due dates. This requires the participant to create their own sense of urgency.

A course, by itself, isn't a community. If community is your goal, a self-study course is not sufficient. If you want to offer a course, you will need to develop a community strategy that's connected to it.

Your course and cohort strategy can include a variety of methods, such as live office hours or coworking sessions to bring members together. You might also consider designing a pairing or accountability program to keep participants on track.

The challenge with this structure is that unless you have a large audience and a community manager to support them, you won't be able to retain your members for long. This is because while they might come to a community for your content, but they stay because of the connections they make and the relationships they build by going through something together.

Creating a sense of community with self-study participants isn't impossible, but it takes effort to sustain. Members like something new or special. If you aren't going to provide them with another opportunity—say, working with you after they finish the course—they will not know what to do next. Worse yet, most people don't even finish online courses and struggle to stay on track with their education goals. With no deadline, there's no reason to hurry up and finish it, and they may later decide they don't need it anymore and leave the community. All these things are unknown until you talk to your members. This takes time from your other daily activities, which is why I mentioned the need to hire support for your course as it launches and grows.

An Immersive, Time-Based Course

An immersive, time-based course or cohort offers students individual teacher support, group coaching, and structured course materials with discussions.

This structure has a set timeframe (i.e., eight weeks, twelve weeks, etc.) and is designed to offer students access to the host and each other to provide a way to share their experiences while working through the course.

The difference between an immersive course and a self-study course is that with an immersive course, individuals meet at a specific time for additional group support. Some programs might also offer individual sessions to members if the subject matter is complex, or the members need additional private coaching.

A Coaching Program

A coaching cohort is team-facilitated by the members sharing their own personal experiences, resources, and feedback during virtual sessions. The point is that members are learning together, not simply going to office hours to ask the leader a question.

Typically, someone hosts coaching call sessions, so the students can drop in to receive support when they need it. If you have a coaching practice and want to offer a group session along with a course, it is an option I've seen work well for a variety of coaches.

Lisa Pepper-Satkin, host of Own Your Brilliance and a Certified Dare to Lead™ Facilitator, leads a weekly group to help women move out of their own way and step into the best version of themselves. Lisa hired me to help her move the coaching program online. We decided to offer a program exclusively for her clients and add an online community element that gave them opportunities to connect between each coaching session. Members found it valuable to be able to regularly check in and reconnect with each other.

A Mastermind Group

The group I led for community builders used a mastermind group structure. It offered a virtual call each week to workshop community-building challenges. In addition, we kept each other accountable for making progress on our community concept, community structure, and community strategy. We stuck together for six months to offer encouragement and support.

This group later developed into a more formal mastermind cohort. This structure included weekly coaching sessions and chances for members to present their community launch or relaunch plans, which we called being in the "growth seats." This gave them an opportunity to gain valuable feedback about pricing, structure, features, and benefits.

Over three months, we focused on different aspects of community building, including concept, strategy, structure, design, and development. At the end of the ninety days, I asked the members to provide feedback about the program.

Here's what some members said after the conclusion of the ninety-day mastermind:

* "I think at every meeting, we should commit to completing a specific task before the next meeting and somehow be held accountable."
* "I think offering to teach a skill (like course building or engagement or onboarding) would be helpful, then having the mastermind as a bonus to anyone who does a paid class."
* "This mastermind is a great place where you meet professionals that are on the same path as you. This is a place where you learn, get ideas, connect, build friendships and business relationships, and grow as a person and as a professional."
* "The mastermind helped me attract and engage new members, feel inspired by the group's examples, and create achievable goals."
* "Having a place to give and receive support with others who are also hoping to build a community on the same platform is invaluable."

From that experience, I redesigned the program and built out guides (discussed in later chapters) to provide the accountability which had been lacking in the first version. When you can, basing your own structure on feedback from members is always a good idea, as it helps you *and* them.

A Challenge

A few clients I've worked with have decided to host challenges at different times in their community. Sometimes a challenge can reinvigorate passive members, and other times it can help a new community get off the ground. The basis of a challenge is that it allows members to take action and compete against each other in a game that sometimes—but not always—has a winner.

Elisha from The Mindful Living Collective decided he wanted to kick off his new community structure with a twenty-one-day meditation challenge that encouraged members to join the new daily meditations, which were called "The Daily Dose." Led by trained facilitators, these featured guided meditations and brief check-ins. Because we had previously surveyed his members, we were able to quickly identify the ideal time to host the challenge.

We compiled quotes, phrases, and inspirational images to schedule a post for each day. Then, we invited members to join the challenge. This inspired action in passive members of the community and encouraged active members to participate in new ways.

The community already had a forum for conversation, so we prompted participants to share what it was like to attend the Daily Dose, either before or after the meditation. We also let them know it was okay to only show up when they could. This level of engagement helped build more authentic interest for the program and was also an effective way to help members feel heard, seen, and valued.

During the challenge, we notified members that the community structure would be changing. To offer a better experience and bring in trained facilitators, the community would shift from a free space to a donation-based membership. Acting as a community transition manager, my role was to inform people of the changes and guide as many members as possible to the donation page. I emphasized how much we valued their time (and the facilitators' contributions) and let them know if they chose not to participate in the donation model, they would be removed from the community, which then had over 7,000 members. The challenge inspired those who did see the notifications to reactivate their experience and recommit to a life of mindful living.

Annual, Semiannual, and Monthly Memberships

An online membership that requires members to pay at the door means you need to have already won them over and have their trust. Memberships come with a sense of belonging, and people must feel that sense of belonging when they arrive at your website, or they must already know a few members, or they are unlikely to join.

* ☆ An example of an *annual membership* is the Chamber of Commerce; if you are a member, you are invited to events to support your local community, and your name is listed in the mailer sent out to all the local residents.
* ☆ *Semi-annual coaching programs* run anywhere from six weeks to two years and are another community membership option. Many coaches have said that a six-month program works best for both their personal schedule and the client's ability to commit. The decision on the date is up to you.
* ☆ *Monthly memberships,* offered by a host, require members to pay monthly dues to access content, member directories, private chats, resources, and more, depending on the terms and conditions of that membership.

Creator Community Monthly Memberships, Collaborations

A new term has emerged: the creator community. As a visual artist and creator, my content includes photographs, podcast episodes, blog posts, and audio recordings. I can repurpose any of these into a course, or I can collaborate with fellow business owners looking to rebrand to create additional revenue streams. Those revenue streams could include a membership model to support my work.

I'm not alone in wanting to somehow monetize my work. There are 200 million creators, according to the 2022 Creator Report. I've struggled to make it as a creator because of the sheer determination and energy it takes to consistently publish high-quality work without cash. It has taken me years to pivot my business strategy and rework my pricing, offers, and services in hopes that my audience will wake up and support my work. That's when I learned about the creator community economy and discovered the world of community building, with people who, just like me, wanted to bring together people to create transformative experiences.

The modern-day type of free exposure for creatives is social media. The challenge is to gain followers, and thereby, status, but no one has ever really understood what that means for us. Frankly, it now seems creators are simply the user generators companies prey on for their content. The truth is that social media algorithms use your content to push advertisements to your audience, or else they work against you.

The world undervalues many creators trying to make a living at what they do best. Yes, there are creators who have reached the top, hit six figures, and found success. In the Creator Report, forty-eight percent of creators who make $100,000 to $500,000 a year spend greater than ten hours a week on content creation.

So, a new idea emerged. YouTubers, podcasters, and creatives in many other fields across the globe decided to go directly to their audience and stop paying to be seen. Some even started to connect with their subscribers and began building relationships with them.

1. *A YouTube influencer* needs to have an audience of 10,000 followers to launch a membership for a low monthly pricing structure.
2. *A niche content creator* can be described as an expert within an industry who has a specific skill or talent that is unique and needed within that industry.
3. *A community creator* is looking for an opportunity to bring clients, friends, or followers into an online community membership for the purpose of earning recurring revenue.

These are only a few examples of the ways creators are making money online, and the reason it is so hard to figure out what is right for you is because there are so many options and with them, a lot of distractions.

Any business owner knows the key to entrepreneurship is diversifying their income and getting their audience to support them directly with member-supported community apps such as Patreon, Podfan, Buy Me a Coffee, among others. As you can see, there is so much to consider when launching an online community, and knowing how to raise money or garner investors is key to a successful community and business. Next up is a client example of a mother-daughter podcasting team that grew an online business and community using mindful membership strategies.

Mindful Memberships and Monetization Strategies

As a podcaster, I can relate to the desire to be compensated for the time and effort that goes into putting together a podcast. While it is much easier than a decade ago, the economy still doesn't recognize creative content such as interviews or educational audio stories, courses, or case studies in the mainstream consumer market.

Most podcasters want to monetize their podcast as soon as they realize it isn't simply sitting down and talking into a mic. Podcasting involves editing the raw content—which could be audio, video, or both—and uploading that content as files. In addition to editing, a podcast producer spends time creating captions, titles, tags, and social media graphics to promote episodes.

If you have an interview-style podcast, you also need a producer to manage your booking schedule and to maintain a flow of guests for your podcast. If you have the capital to do so, you can hire companies that offer these support services. If you don't, this is the work you'll be doing as a podcaster. Once podcasters find out how much work is involved, many aren't as excited to continue recording without some type of financial resources such as a sponsor, investors, or supporters.

Emma and Mary, hosts of *The Good Dirt* podcast, had supporters, but they wanted more. The mother-daughter duo opened the ALMANAC, a private paid community for those who want to practice slow living and share their skills. When I worked with Emma and Mary, they asked me to help them restructure the community to improve members' experiences. From conversations with their members, we received actionable feedback that we implemented into their community strategy.

The new membership model we developed looked like this:

* A core community staple will be the slow living challenge in January.
* Podcast supporters will receive extra content.
* Members can volunteer to lead a skill share session to benefit the community.
* Emma will host a three-month Artist Way study group (additional cost to members).
* Mary will host a three-month Regenerative Gardening program (additional cost to members).

To be mindful about your membership means you'll need to think about how you will fund each phase of your community launch strategy (more on this later).

I learned the hard way—after spending too much time and energy trying to sell low-priced memberships before I had an audience—that building an online membership can take anywhere from one to three years. This average is based on an entrepreneur or business owner who is hosting a community as an additional revenue stream, not as their main offer or income.

Now, this really varies from one community to another, so it really depends on several factors, but overall, the more specific you are—the more niche and exclusive—the faster you will see financial success.

The following timeline is based on my own experience and what I've learned working with over sixty clients, in addition to industry reports and data that have stated community member adoption can take longer depending on the resources you have available and the time you can dedicate to nurturing the growth of your community. It is like a garden; it needs water, sun, and care.

1. The first phase is about building the foundation of who you are (your brand), what you do (your services or products), and how people will get to know you (how you will market these). People need to know you and what it is you do so that *you can be known as the go-to.*

2. The second phase is focused on building meaningful relationships with your ideal members and getting to know them, while they, in turn, get to know you. That is when you discover what problems they have, how they've tried to solve them in the past, and if they've ever joined an online community to help navigate this challenge. It is critical to customize your community concept for your ideal members, and if you discover that the problem your ideal member faces is something they don't want to workshop with others, it is a sign that a community is not a good fit for this problem. Try again.

3. The third phase begins when you've started to build a super fan base, and people ask to work or collaborate with you in some way. They want to know what you know or reach some goal you've been able to achieve, but you have to tell them that. You will need to convert these followers into true community members who want to be a part of something bigger than themselves, join a movement, find a tribe, feel a sense of belonging, and so much more.

The next chapter will focus on discovering your ideal members. Knowing them will help you move through these phases faster and will aid your success when you launch your program, course, or membership.

Chapter Snapshot

* ✦ An online community structure encompasses the design of a community's features, member benefits, strategy, vision, and purpose established by the community host.
* ✦ Community culture is the way you tell members how to feel seen, valued, and heard. It's written into your community guidelines, demonstrated in your member testimonials, and expressed by members when they talk about your community to others.
* ✦ I've offered six possible ways to run your community, including self-study, interactive courses, time-based courses, mastermind groups, challenges, and memberships.

Action Items

Identify your community architecture: Decide if you want a cohort-based or membership-based model.

Cohort-Based
1. Self-study course with a cohort
2. Immersive course with a cohort
3. Coaching group
4. Mastermind cohort
5. Challenge cohort

Creator Community Memberships
1. YouTube influencer (funded by brand deals)
2. Niche content creator (creator-to-creator marketplace, business-to-business marketplace, software as a service)
3. Community creator (memberships, courses, masterminds, or a combination of revenue streams from online stores and sponsorship)

Below are some types of memberships with which you might be familiar:
1. Podcast supporter memberships
2. Skill-sharing memberships
3. Support communities
4. Educational communities
5. Networking communities
6. Technology communities
7. Industry-specific communities
8. Special interest communities
9. Change communities (leading a movement)
10. Creative, entrepreneurial, collaborative, and resource-sharing communities such as collectives of experts or specialists

Questions to Consider

What kind of structure best suits the problem your members are trying to solve?

What's the best way for your members to meet, connect, or collaborate?

How many online communities are you in, and why do you participate?

SECTION 2:

Ideal Members, Validation, Planning

Mt. Sanitas, Boulder, Colorado

"How are you going to find out about things if you don't ask questions?"

— L.M. Montgomery

CHAPTER 4

Discover Your Ideal Members

When I joined the Location Indie community, I transformed from someone who worked at a corporate job and wanted to travel more, to someone who is location independent. This didn't happen over-night; it took two-and-a-half years of learning from and building relationships with community members. The best part of an online community is finding people who simply "get you," right from the beginning. My friends in the community were also going through the same things at the same time. They, too, wanted to become location independent and travel, and we transformed together.

Over the same period of time, while I was building my business, my friends in the community were marketing and promoting their services or products to the masses and trying to make their living as creators or virtual assistants. Some did have full-time remote jobs, but most members of Location Indie dreamed of quitting their nine-to-five jobs to start online businesses.

If I had known the term then, I would have realized I was Loca-tion Indie's ideal member, a person who fits the profile of the community creator's target audience. They have a problem the creator can help them overcome with their community's assistance, support, knowledge, network, or resources.

The friends I met in Location Indie are still among my best friends. I see them on Instagram, Facebook, or LinkedIn, and I support them anytime they are doing something amazing. I know that, if I needed it, they would pick up the phone and talk with me.

You never know the magic you can create by bringing people together. The more you know about your members, the better you will engage them. Even if your community never has in-person gatherings, find a way to connect with your members.

Start with the IDEA™:
Identify, Discover, Evaluate, Assemble

One of the most challenging aspects of community building is finding and reaching your ideal members. You'll need to give them good reasons why your community deserves their time, energy, money, and attention.

To gain members who are committed to your community's purpose and who are interested in showing up to collaborate, you'll need to have a few strategic elements in place. When you launch a community, you will want to make sure you invite the right people into the room—people who will participate, show up to events, share resources, and support other members. Community building is all about building relationships among members.

To help your community concept make its way to the finish line, I developed the IDEA™ framework: Identify, Discover, Evaluate, and Assemble. The following section is a blueprint for you to streamline your community-building journey. However, before we jump in, I want to emphasize that the foundation of a community strategy is essential.

Doing this work upfront *will save you time and money*. You may have heard startups and founders say, "Fail fast. Fail frequently."

In a 2018 *Forbes* article, Dan Pontefract wrote, "When executives institute a 'fail fast, fail often' mantra, they must ensure it is not at the expense of creative or critical thinking."

Identify

The first step in building an online community is to *know who you are bringing together.* This can be the most challenging part because your community concept may serve many different people. The key to creating a sense of belonging in an online community is to clearly define who it's for and who it isn't. When others hear about your community, they should know easily if they belong.

Community is about exclusion, which can be counterintuitive, since you will define who, essentially, "doesn't belong." Still, allow the core values and purpose to guide you to a clear vision of who the community is for. The clearer this is to you and others, the more successful your community launch will be. In *The Art of Gathering: How We Meet and Why It Matters,* Priya Parker writes, "In a world of infinite choices, choosing one thing is the revolutionary act. Imposing that restriction is actually liberating."

Looking back, it is clear the purpose of Location Indie was to gather those interested in working remotely while traveling the world. In a pre-pandemic society, this concept wasn't widely accepted. At least, I didn't know anyone else who was interested in, or pursuing this lifestyle. I needed to find people online who were living the way I wanted to live, since it wasn't being modeled in my current network.

Their tagline calls directly to their audience: A community of people helping each other kick ass in business and travel. The wording inspires working professionals who desire connection and encouragement. Going deeper, the landing page of Location Indie lists member benefits. It affirms the problems this community solves and for whom.

The more specific you can be about who your community is for, what members do together, and how this helps them achieve their goals, the more your message will resonate with your ideal members.

Discover

When working with clients, I am often asked about what "discovery" means when it comes to launching an online community. It is a process in which you *become curious about who will make up your online community*. It means getting to know actual humans and requires a few skills, all of which can be learned, developed, or resourced.

Many leaders make the mistake of assuming they know the best way to solve a problem. They don't conduct interviews, do research, or talk to real people, and they lean heavily on customer avatars (fake people profiles). The reason for this varies from one creator to the next, but most new community builders don't have the courage to speak to their ideal members. Instead, they talk to the masses of social media, which ends up speaking to a lot of people rather than one specific person.

Discovery interviews can help you answer your questions before you launch a community. In the next chapter, I'll discuss why validation of your idea is so important, but this chapter will focus on having conversations with your members.

I recommend speaking on a phone call or a Zoom call with at least ten ideal members, people who have expressed interest by answering your social media posts, responding to an advertisement, or filling out an application to be a part of your upcoming program.

Consider:

   ☆ What's the common thread that connects your ideal members?

☆ Can you picture activities they'd be passionate about participating in?
☆ In what ways might they share the community with friends, family, or colleagues?

An Ideal Member Conversation

The best way to build relationships is to simply speak one-on-one with your ideal members. You may not have prioritized this due to time constraints, but skipping this step will force you to make a lot of assumptions.

If you haven't asked an ideal community member about their challenges, needs, and goals, you won't know if the solution you are building will be useful to them. If you're unsure who your ideal members are, start with your existing network. Open up your email and phone contacts, Facebook friends, LinkedIn connections, or Instagram followers and find ten to twenty people within your network who best fit your ideal member.

Then, invite them to a conversation. Maybe it's in person, or maybe suggest a virtual coffee that allows them to join you from the comfort of their home.

Ask them where they spend time online. Find out if they are active in any online communities, have taken any online courses, or have been a part of any group programs. Learn about their current lifestyles. Ask them to consider where they are in relation to the problem your community will solve and where they'd like to be in a year. Connect the dots between their experiences and others like them and explain how an online community might be beneficial. It's proven that big lifestyle shifts are more easily achieved with like-minded people supporting each other.

Validate their pain and frustration. Ask them why this shift needs to happen sooner, rather than later. If possible, find out why they want to change, if they've tried in the past, or if they know of others who've been successful. Then, verify that they are interested in changing as they may not be ready. If they're not ready, that's okay! Your goal is to attract those who are willing and able to fully participate.

Be strategic about your questions but authentic about your interest. This is a template for speaking with your members, but this is not what you should copy and paste into an email. I work with clients to customize these interviews, but since you are reading this and not working with me right now (unless you are), you will need to know how to fill in the blanks.

To collect the data needed to send out these kinds of messages, you'll need to have a strong relationship established with them already.

While social media and websites serve the masses, a community is a way to go deeper. By focusing on your ideal member and getting to know the exact person who could make up your first beta launch, you will expedite the sales process.

Here's what I mean. Most business books discuss the "know, like, and trust factors," which I've mentioned earlier, with the add-on of needing to develop deeper relationships with collaborators.

Spend time getting to know your ideal members and approach the conversation strategically, focused on the key community questions listed below:

- ☆ Do they have the problem you think they have?
- ☆ Do they want your help?
- ☆ Do they want help from a community of peers?
- ☆ Do they want to be a part of an online community?
- ☆ Have they been a part of an online community? If so, when and where?

During the call or meetup, you can decide on the best approach with these individuals, but you'll want to find out the answers to the questions above and confirm they will be a fit for the community concept you are envisioning.

The downside to doing ideal member interviews is they do take a lot of time. You will need to block out time for the following tasks:

1. Research your network for potential ideal members.
2. Identify at least twenty people who fit your ideal member profile.
3. Personally reach out to each individual with a warm reconnection note to see if they'd be willing to chat with you.

Surveys Save Time and Help Creators with Large Audiences Confirm Assumptions

Suppose you've been in business for a while and have established an audience through social media, an email list, or networking groups. In that case, a survey may help you identify the best people to speak with before you reach out to arrange coffee chats. You can refine your list of potential ideal members by posing questions that best align with your community concept.

Here's how you can craft and carry out a survey to help you produce a refined list:

1. Write out your community purpose, vision, and mission using the information you know about your existing audience.
2. Pull testimonials and emails from previous clients to find commonalities among these individuals based on their needs and challenges which can then align them with the benefits of the community.
3. Decide how your community concept can meet those needs and challenges. Rewrite each problem statement as a question. For example, if a past client has said they struggled with getting something done, ask, "Would

you be interested in an accountability group to help you accomplish this task?"

4. Turn your community's mission into a written statement that can serve as a call to action for the people who need it. Give the viewer a picture of what information you're seeking, the people from whom you're seeking information, and *what's in it for them*. Make sure to include how they can learn when your community will launch, should they be interested.

5. Finalize a list of the most active audience members and send a survey with fewer than ten questions. The questions should be short and relevant to their needs, not yours.

SURVEY TIPS

- ☆ Have a clearly defined purpose that can be easily understood in thirty seconds or less.
- ☆ Make it easy to complete in five minutes or less.
- ☆ Keep questions brief and to the point (multiple choice, yes-or-no).
- ☆ Don't forget to ask if you can contact them for further discussion.
- ☆ Give them incentive to complete the survey (a discount or special offer).
- ☆ Assign a deadline to encourage immediate action.

Hire an Interviewer

Finally, if there are time constraints in place and a budget available, I recommend bringing in an expert who can ask questions for you. Depending on each interviewer's method, you may or may not have a role in the process.

As a former journalist and reporter, I am skilled at asking questions, communicating clearly, and uncovering hidden gems during interviews. In 2021, I was hired by Paul Bradly to help him conduct interviews; together, we crafted effective questions and found the best candidates for interviews, so we could validate our assumptions around the problems his new community would solve. I later interviewed him for *The Community Strategy Podcast*, and here's what he had to say about discovery interviews:

From "Episode 56: Earning your members' trust with Paul Bradley":

 "If you can get people to talk to you, it will be instrumental in helping craft the community cadence. The questions that we used in our discovery process, which was hugely successful, taught me so much about the needs of our ideal members. If you create what they need, they'll start to engage, and then once they're engaging, they'll be telling you what they constantly need just with their engagement. Regardless of what your community is doing, whether it's a huge corporate thing or trying to get people in small groups to pay your subscription fee, it's all about earning trust."

Paul later referred me to his colleague, Theresa Anderson, who hired me to conduct discovery interviews as the company Agorapulse was preparing to launch a new product. We worked together to develop questions that would ensure the product launch would succeed.

She wanted to work with me to have an *unbiased individual asking these questions* and to gain a different perspective. I knew nothing about their software and wasn't among their target audience—social media managers. Additionally, I brought to the interviews a willingness to learn about their challenges, experiences, and needs.

Though we began with assumptions about what social media managers experience, we made sure our questions didn't reflect any bias or preconceptions. If survey questions unintentionally influence people to answer a certain way, the data can't be fully trusted. As we discovered, many social media managers were doing a lot more than simply reviewing data and reporting to leadership.

We also learned that, thanks to their widely varying roles, "engagement" in the Agorapulse community meant different things to different people.

The product that Agorapulse was launching was a dashboard for customer metrics. In other words, it was a place for social-media managers to see all analytics in one place. Theresa was able to gain valuable insights from our survey. Her biggest discovery was that the dashboard would not only be convenient for customers, but it would also save them (and their company) time and money. Because Agorapulse had been spending so much time building, launching, and marketing, they welcomed this confirmation that the tool would land well with their target audience.

From "Episode 73: The Value of Discovery Work with Theresa Anderson":

"I feel like discovery doesn't always get its due as far as how important it is when you're doing pretty much anything. It's easy to get in your own bubble."

What you need before hiring an interviewer:

⋆ Know your expectations and ensure the interviewer understands what you need. Set up a meeting to review the goals, timeline, and outcomes before the interviews are scheduled.

⋆ Make sure the interviewer has the full picture of your survey's purpose. Let the interviewer know the kinds of data you're seeking. For example, if you're asking about a community you want to build, clarify that you're looking for honest responses about your customer's journey, past experiences in communities, and how your customer might want to connect with others in your community.

☆ Ensure the interviewer has experience developing unbiased questions and can gather neutral information. If you have an existing audience, especially, you may need to seek respondents with different perspectives. Let's say you're surveying fifteen to twenty people, including past clients, but also those who've engaged with your content but haven't yet hired you or bought your product.

If someone's experience with you wasn't positive, consider asking for their opinion, too. Understanding why your solution *didn't* ultimately help them can be just as useful as glowing reviews.

Chapter Snapshot

☆ The IDEA framework can help you clarify your community concept prior to launch. The framework is Identify, Discover, Evaluate, and Assemble. Evaluate and Assemble will be discussed in Chapter 5.

☆ Be intentional about how you request an interview or survey. Draft a brief query which clearly states what you're asking of them. Be sure to state how the conversation will benefit them by including their values and goals in the wording of your request.

☆ You have three options for discovery: conducting ideal-member interviews, conducting ideal-member surveys, or hiring an interviewer.

Action Items

1. Decide how you will identify your ideal members. If they fall into categories, list them.
2. Block off time on your calendar and set a deadline for the interviews or survey.
3. Dedicate time to refining your community purpose statement.
4. Review member benefits.
5. Ask for help with the interviews. If there is a budget available, hire an expert.

Questions to Consider

What questions do you have for potential members?

What option for discovery best suits your current goals: ideal-member interviews or a survey?

If you were to reach out to current clients as potential ideal members, who comes to mind?

Acadia National Park, Maine

"We cannot change what we are not aware of, and once we are aware, we cannot help but change."

— Sheryl Sandberg

CHAPTER 5

Validate Your Community

In the summer of 2021, I took a hiking trip to Acadia National Park in Maine. It was a nice day, and I headed up the trail not considering the weather. After an hour, I ran into two people hiking down who informed me about a quickly approaching storm.

My goal was to reach the top to capture a wide shot of the region, but I wasn't as fit as I'd been a few years prior. I continued anyway, now actively aware of my pace. Moving faster, I made it to the top and got my shot, but I didn't waste time; I made sure to hustle on my way back down. I lucked out and didn't feel raindrops until reaching a lower section of the trail. Thanks to my fellow hikers, I had better information and could adapt my actions. I still achieved my goal, but I'd approached the experience differently than when I had begun. Those hikers made all the difference, and I was so grateful for them!

In the last chapter, I introduced the IDEA™ framework: Identify, Discover, Evaluate, and Assemble. So far, we've discussed Identify and Discover. This chapter will dive deep into evaluating your discovery findings and preparing *to assemble your community* based on the validation your members have provided.

IDEA™ Framework: Evaluate

In Chapter 4, *Discover Your Ideal Members*, we discussed how the Identify step helps us to define who our community is for and how the Discover process allows you to learn about your future members and add value to the community for both you and them.

Now, let's move on to the next part of the IDEA framework. You might be thinking that at this point, we'll jump into data, metrics, and spreadsheets. Instead, we'll look at a simple way to review your community discovery based on the three options outlined in the previous chapter.

The responses you collected in the discovery process will give you what you *need* to determine the next step in your community-building process. Because community building takes work and time, reviewing your results carefully will prevent wasted resources.

IDEAL MEMBER CONVERSATIONS

Once you've had conversations with the ten to twenty people who best fit your ideal member, it will be time to review what you've learned.

MEMBER EXPERIENCE

When speaking with your ideal members, you'll learn if they have experienced online communities and, if so, how they are currently participating. This will help you identify the best way to provide your members with a unique and memorable experience.

PERSONAL CHALLENGES

Depending on how open and willing they are to share their challenges, you may learn how your ideal members have overcome past roadblocks and moved through difficult times. You can ask them who they leaned on most during those times and discover if a community would help them in solving a problem they have right now.

TRANSFORMATION AND READINESS

During chats with ideal members, you'll identify critical aspects of the community structure that can inspire transformation. When reviewing the notes from your conversations with ideal members, think about their journeys. Look for evidence that they want to solve the problem your community addresses.

For example, if your community will help people who struggle with procrastination, note when interviewees mention this issue, such as a time when they delayed action. Pay attention to how long it took them to address that delay. Look for examples of them putting effort into overcoming procrastination. If they don't mention that they have this exact problem, they may not be ready to change.

IDEAL MEMBER SURVEY

You've sent out the survey, and now it's time to look at the results. Depending on the size of your audience, you may have hundreds of responses to review or maybe only a dozen. Whatever the number, set aside adequate time to review the responses.

Using your available digital tools, create a spreadsheet or notes document to help you organize the results. For example, Google Forms can automatically add responses to a spreadsheet, separating each prompt into individual columns.

Key Themes to Examine

Start reviewing individual responses to see how they chose to respond or if they left things blank. As you move from one person to the next, you will start to see repetitive themes emerge.

THE PROBLEM

As you reflect on the responses, pay attention to the problems they share with you. Ask yourself if the same problem comes up repeatedly. Note each instance and look for commonalities. When patterns emerge, you'll know you're onto something.

THE SOLUTION

If you've found that people resonate with the problem, the next critical factor is to understand how they want to solve it. Some people deeply desire spending time on personal development by reading alone, journaling, and connecting with nature. Suppose your respondents say they've attempted to solve this problem independently but don't have the motivation, determination, or discipline to hold themselves accountable. In that case, a community could be a good fit for them. If they express interest in helping others navigate this challenge, a community will be a beautiful fit. If you hear people say they aren't ready or don't want to help others, they may have more success solving the problem independently.

MEMBER EXPERIENCE

The members of your online community want to have a good experience, and you want them to as well, so make sure you leave them wanting more at each step in their journey. Learn what they really enjoy doing together and allow them to contribute ideas for new experiences. Find different ways to connect with them. For example, if your community is focused on business networking, it would be nice to share what your members do for fun when they aren't trying to gain customers or clients. Search for fun experiences you can bring to the community such as game nights, watch parties, and scavenger hunts. I've been part of an online community that conducted a murder mystery night! At the end of the day, your members want to have fun, and so do you!

HIRE AN INTERVIEWER

If you've decided to hire someone to conduct interviews, make sure you've taken the necessary steps to align your goals and expectations of the outcome with the interviewer. Tell them the key themes about which you're seeking information.

Hiring an interviewer is a great way to save time and money by letting yourself be on the sidelines. Once the interviewer has completed the interviews and provided you with the responses, ask any questions you have about their process and findings. Do they have notes or additional feedback? Have your expectations been met?

By the end of this project, you should have gathered usable testimonials, critical feedback on your community concept, and content to start building your offer. You should have what you need to develop sales copy and move to prelaunch, which I'll cover in the next chapter. The IDEA framework also continues in Chapter 6, *Plan Your Community*, with Assemble, which is the first step of your prelaunch.

Chapter Snapshot

☆ This chapter focuses on *evaluating* your results from ideal
member interviews, surveys, or your interview expert.

☆ The conversations and responses you collect will be the
information you *need* to decide on the next step. Community building takes work and time, but reviewing your
results will give you a clear picture.

☆ Focus on gathering information about members' experiences. When speaking with your ideal members, you'll
learn how they have experienced online communities
and how they have participated.

Action Items

1. Review the responses from your interviews or survey. Whether you've worked on your own or with someone you hired, be sure to review the feedback in detail.
2. Look for problems that align with your solution. Identify the challenges your people face, so you can structure your community to best solve those problems.
3. By this point, you should be able to compare your community concept with your ideal member responses.

Questions to Consider

What did you learn about your ideal members from your conversations, survey, or research?

Do they want to work on this over a short or long period of time?

What are their expectations about the community and its outcome?

Red Rocks Amphitheatre, Denver, Colorado

"Alone we can do so little; together we can do so much."
— Helen Keller

CHAPTER 6

Plan Your Community

Before my trip to Denver, one of the hosts of Location Indie shared a story about doing the "hard things" in life. Sometimes, the things that seem banal or draining—like setting up a website, developing a marketing plan, or doing taxes—are the very things that move us forward. Over time, a tagline developed in the Location Indie community: I Tackled the Buffalo. Basically, you did something you didn't want to do. I mean, who wants to tackle a buffalo anyway?

Sometimes that *hard thing* is something we deeply want, such as quitting a job we hate to explore a new career. Other times, it's something that doesn't even sound fun, such as sending an invoice, organizing files, or increasing prices.

When I received my t-shirt with the phrase, "I tackled the buffalo," I realized something. *My very presence at this event* was an achievement. By attending, I'd stepped out of my comfort zone toward the life I truly wanted. I wanted to capture this experience of bravery and joy, so later that day on a beautiful hike with my newfound Location Indie friends, I asked one of them to photograph me.

In this chapter, I'll cover the final phase of the IDEA framework: Assemble. As you embark on this phase, remember the value of doing the hard stuff. Make no mistake; launching a community takes time and effort. For many of us, the planning parts are the "less fun" ones. However, doing the hard parts of community building is the only way to keep it alive. For me, it was the only way to avoid going back to a job. It's not all "fun," and it is work, but it doesn't have to be stressful.

The IDEA™ Framework: Assemble Your Community Strategy

By this point, we've discussed the first three stages of the IDEA framework: Identify, Discover, and Evaluate. Now it's time to talk about how to *assemble* your launch plan. Planning when, how, and where to launch an online community usually takes about three to six months; I recommend spending one month on each of the first three phases and a subsequent one to three months assembling your community design and launch plan. This will include preparing for prelaunch, launch, and postlaunch, with time built in for you to beta test the platform.

It can be done faster, or it can take longer, depending on your resources, time, and commitment level. Whatever you do, be sure not to skip this step. Honor it. If you want to rush through it, accept the fact that inadequate strategy leads to unwanted results. Deciding when to launch depends on a few factors and will ultimately be determined by your existing business model. For example, if you have other large launches at the beginning of the year, then simultaneously launching a community will drain your team. The best advice I can give is to think about what has worked for you in the past.

Ray Green, host of the Repeatable Revenue community, worked with me on his launch plan. He decided to bring in current consulting clients and asked them to test out the platform and provide feedback. He learned that the platform he had selected wasn't a good fit for his clients, an insight he wouldn't have gained had he not asked his members to test out the software prior to launching.

From "Episode 59: Find Calm with a slow launch strategy":

 "We invited about twenty people into our premium section to test and slow roll the onboarding. We took feedback from them and set appropriate expectations of it being a beta program."

Tips for Deciding When to Launch

Discuss the community launch with your team to identify when resources will be most available for your project. If you work inside an organization, you'll need support from marketing, sales, and the IT department. If you need to consult legal and financial advisors, do it now.

If you don't have a team or organization, start small with a beta group to test your idea. Five to ten people is enough.

If you're launching a timed program, such as a four-week course or a three-month coaching program, be strategic about when. The least preferable times to launch are in the summer (because many people travel), during the holidays, and at the beginning of the new year. Based on my research, the best time is in the spring or fall.

The steps to launch your community will depend on the structure and strategy you've outlined during the earlier phases. From my experience building over sixty online communities, I can tell you that the "how" came down to what was best for each client.

Some clients started an email list of over 100,000 people, while others had a large social media following. Some didn't have an email list or large audience at all, so they focused on colleagues and established contacts to develop their strategy around those ideal members.

Tips for How and Where to Launch

☆ If you have an established email list and following, you
can start promoting your new program, course, membership, or challenge very early on in the process. You'll
want to tell people what's coming and how they can
learn more.

☆ A splash page, also called a landing page, can be helpful in promoting your community before it launches. If
you plan to do an email newsletter, most software will
provide a landing page option as a feature of your paid
subscription, but you will need to decide what is right
for you.

☆ You can create a business card and share the community
invite link on the back.

☆ Before comparing community platforms or spending
money and time learning new software, I'd recommend
you decide what features and functions you'll need.

Chapter Snapshot

- ☆ You need a team to build a membership community. It can't happen without support from other people.
- ☆ Deciding when to launch your community depends on a few factors and will ultimately be determined by your existing business model.

Action Items

☆ Have an outline of your community launch plan, including dates, tasks, and roles of team members.

Questions to Consider

Do you have resources to support a community launch? If so, list them below:

When would be the best launch time for your schedule and organization? What have you decided or learned about your community strategy or structure?

Did your community structure or strategy change based on your ideal member insights?

If so, how and why?

What do you need before launching your community?

What's a realistic timeframe for this pre launch phase?

SECTION 3:

Building, Launching, and Onboarding

Monarch Butterfly Sanctuary, Central Mexico

*"If you start with a smart strategy, and clear vision, you
will be able to achieve superior results to reach the right
audiences, through the right channels at the right time."*
                                                        — *Germany Kent*

CHAPTER 7

Grow Your Audience

If you have made it this far, you might be surprised to find this chapter so late in the book, but the reason is I believe an audience is simply the people in your existing community who connect to your message and authentic voice.

I started blogging in 2010 on WordPress to build my photography business. At the time, few digital tools existed to help writers market their work. I learned about building a website from CreativeLive, a course platform for creatives.

My first blog story that resonated with a fellow creator was about my trip to Atlanta, Georgia, to visit my cousin. On the trip, several things happened that I ended up blogging about, including when I was almost kicked out of CNN, and when my cousin had a boot put on his car because we didn't feed the parking meter. WordPress has a feature called Reader that allows fellow bloggers to follow each other to offer encouragement. One fellow blogger, David Banks, reached out to tell me he admired my story about Atlanta and wanted to connect.

I found out that Dave was a documentary filmmaker. We stayed in touch, and a few years later, he was writing a book called *Cue the Camels* and wanted my input, feedback, and review.

The feedback I gave him is below:

Laughter is the key to sanity; I learned that long ago. In "Cue the Camels", Dave Banks keeps the reader chuckling with the real stories of what it takes to get the "money shot" in a film documentary. From covering the L.A. Riots in the early '90s with a bodyguard to dodging landmines in Jordan, Banks puts a lighthearted spin on his brushes with death. Between years of shooting in less-than-perfect conditions, Banks takes a "cushy" job on the Tonight Show with Jay Leno. Ironically, he ends up on a stretcher after having an anxiety attack.

Not only does Cue the Camels make for a good laugh, but it also stimulates our sense of adventure and excitement. It inspires all of us to search for the unknown or take risks in life in search of something greater than ourselves. My favorite quote from the book is "It may seem crazy to some that I chose to be freelance or work within such dangerous perimeters. I've never lost my sense of humor or optimism for our world. My goal has always been the same despite any risk: to extract the sublime out of the ordinary, to broach what appear to be cultural barriers, knowing I'll always find some common thread. I regard my work and these journeys as 'tourism for the soul.'"

This review was translated into several languages, and although Dave and I have lost touch as of the time of this writing, I will always have a sweet spot in my heart for the kind stranger who was willing to reach out, give me positive feedback, and ask for help.

Over the years on Facebook, I've posted about job losses, break-ups, and weight struggles. I've also shared my goals, challenges, and how I've overcome my fears. I started blogging after I lost my journalism job, and it helped me process the journey.

When I started blogging, I realized I was sharing my journey, so my friends could see the real me! I've had dozens of people come up to me at festivals, bars, or community events to tell me they like reading my posts and seeing my photos. Since I began traveling more in 2018, some have even said they are living vicariously through me. I've had more than a few people come up to me and say, "I enjoy following you on Facebook," or, "I enjoy your stories."

I now use WordPress to host my content, and I also publish on Medium, which makes it easier for people to subscribe and read my work. In addition to these publishing platforms, I participate in small groups where I can, from time to time, share my experiences, content, and resources and offer my expertise during in-person networking sessions. This is in addition to my social media and email marketing strategies.

In 2020, when I started the process to launch a community, I didn't realize those people would be the first who would show up to support my workshops designed to create calm in daily life. The challenge started when I asked them to pay but wasn't clear in my offer or who it was meant for, so no one signed up.

When I evaluated the people who aligned with my message and saw they had common needs and struggles, I found a way to build a business. Still, it ended up being much different than I thought it would be. So many of the clients I've worked with or people I've talked to speak about community building as a passive income. As I've discussed earlier, a community can't be passive.

Growing Your Audience, Not Selling to Them

Tim Ferriss' *The 4-Hour Work Week* introduced a generation who didn't fit the corporate life mold to an alternative path. Since then, millions of people have fallen prey to this passive income trap that doesn't serve anyone. The truth is that passive income isn't passive. It takes work. If you don't want to do the work, work for someone else, but in no way is there anything passive about entrepreneurship; before you can tackle the passive part, you have to create the products, build the systems, manage the employees, and scale the business to run itself without you, all of which take time, energy, and, of course, money.

Over the past few years, my eyes have been opened by a series of books, documentaries, and reflections on my personal experiences in life and how society has guided my decision-making process. Without money, nothing is possible. That is the reality today, but will it be that way in 100 years? None of us will ever know. However, there's the good news. You are the answer to the problem because your experiences can help others. You've been through challenging times and have come out on the other side!

That's the structure of an ecosystem; we serve the community's needs together by sharing wisdom. This might not sound flashy or fancy, but offering a space for someone to feel seen, valued, and heard, without any expected outcome, is a magical experience.

So, what can you do now if you don't want to build a following on Facebook? You can still build relationships through your network by focusing on the core problems you will solve. Then, find where those people are and meet them there, instead of making them come to you.

Robin Fuller, a client who hired me to organize her courses and content, had built an audience mostly away from social media. She said, "Over the past five years, I have been gradually and slowly building my email list, growing it from twenty-five to 155 people. I know my niche and where to find them, often through speaking at conferences or direct referrals."

Robin is a certified coach who helps pregnancy center directors and leaders through challenges with her programs, courses, and community of peers. She wants to provide an "oasis" of resources for her members. For Robin, every person matters, and she considers relationship building a way to help others, but if they aren't interested, she doesn't take it personally.

"Each of these nonprofit leaders has asked to be added to my list, and I never 'auto-add' anyone. The goal is to grow more relationships with the leaders on my list who know me, like me. I offer occasional free events and keep a mindset of generosity."

Robin doesn't push products, services, or offers on potential clients. Instead, she focuses on building relationships and providing value, so they know she cares. "The most important thing I have realized? There is often no 'quick and fast' way to make money. It takes time and long-term consistency."

There's a Difference Between a Lifestyle and an Idea

If your goal is to become location independent, it will take more than an idea to start your business and gain enough income to travel while working. Vanessa Codorniu, founder of The Biz Bruja, has worked for over twenty-seven years as a professional psychic, hypnotherapist, teacher, and shamanic practitioner. She has cultivated transformative experiences that yield practical tools to help individuals find their true selves.

An Argentine American from New York City, Vanessa started building her business with small, in-person circles that stemmed from her lifestyle and the desire to continue growing and learning with others.

"I've learned to lead in a way that is not controlling; it's not hierarchical. It started for free, but when I lost three jobs in four years, I needed to find additional revenue and decided that I wanted to go full-time with this business," Vanessa said.

In 2012, Vanessa started researching online business and marketing.

After years of leading small workshops and sharing her journey with others, she decided she wanted to reach more people online. She describes herself as a "human generator."

Similar to the term "multipotentialite," Vanessa's term is a way of saying, "I have a lot of interests and am good at a lot of things, not only one or two." Vanessa is the same; she is a master at finding something she loves and going after it with admirable strength and grit.

Back then, there were very few digital tools or systems for the kind of work Vanessa wanted to do, but she found she could use Skype and emails to connect with her new audience and share with them upcoming courses, programs, and workshops. Since she began podcasting, writing, blogging, and leading in-person circles—virtually since the pandemic—she has been successful in growing her audience and, in 2020, had her best revenue year ever.

Vanessa credits her success during the pandemic to trying new things and having a loyal following that was in place before the pandemic. Instead of resting, like some of her peers, she rose to the occasion and did the work of building her online presence.

"People tell me things they haven't told their therapist, so they need to be able to trust me, and that doesn't just happen; it takes time. I gave my time every week, offering gathering circles for men and women, many who were unemployed creatives who didn't have a job to go to, so they showed up," she said.

In 2014, Vanessa dedicated time to learn about passive income and built a self-study course to see if she could engage learners without being really active herself. She discovered that three weeks into the course, the learner would often quit. However, when she showed up on a live call, more learners would stay and complete the course. Therefore, she knows her content is valuable, but she is still trying to find an offer that balances her time and her resources, while ensuring members feel seen, heard, and valued.

Pre Launch Tips From Leaders in the Community Industry

I've met some of the best people through Meetup! If you're unfamiliar with this platform, it's a fantastic resource for meeting people with targeted interests. If you are considering starting a Meetup, check out which groups are available in your area and when they meet. You might be able to validate if there's a need that the existing groups in your community don't serve.

On *The Community Strategy Podcast*, I interviewed David Siegel, the CEO of Meetup ("Episode 98: Keep Connected"). During that conversation, he recommended finding two or three people you can build a community with, so you don't have to do it alone. "Too often, new community builders take on too much initially. Create a leadership team, and it will grow from there."

Let's look at a couple of founders who built communities from the ground up.

Joanne Flynn Black, Founder of LaunchB4, helps new business owners "feel ready" to launch. In 2020, after having worked in program management for companies including WeWork and Deloitte, she opened her own community. When I met Joanne, I was enjoying a group called "Vision to Action Board" within her community.

The group stemmed from the idea that photos and words can help us positively change our lives. However, there's a disconnect. While it's nice to have a poster that represents the changes you want to make, it can be hard to actually make them happen. Joanne's group met weekly to share their visions and action items, which they plotted on an online project-management tool, Trello Board. Some of the best advice Joanne shares is about knowing you already have everything you need.

> *Just be confident in what you already have and get out there and do it! When launching a new membership, keep it as simple as possible. You don't want your members coming in and feeling overwhelmed. Have them come into your membership feeling ready to dive in!*

On the other side of the community-building spectrum is Matthew Grande, cofounder of Careerage. He tried launching a community but closed it after learning some hard lessons. "I screwed up trying to coach people, create content, and form a community. As one person, it was too much, so I closed the community and focused solely on one-on-one coaching. It has been beneficial to focus, but I want to have a community again someday."

Chapter Snapshot

* Meet people where they are and lower your own expectations about the journey. It doesn't have to be perfect.
* Decide on the experience you want to have with the community and what the member experience will be like.
* Consider the more profound meaning of this work for you and the impact it will have on the community members.
* If you don't have an existing audience, identify how you've connected with others in communities.

Action Items

1. Research existing communities—Meetup, Facebook, or in your local area. Think about how yours could be different. Also consider how you might interact with them most effectively.
2. Develop your pre launch member experience based on what you already know about your ideal members, your personal experiences, and what you're excited about doing.
3. Challenge yourself to create fun and inspiring experiences in the pre launch phase.

Questions to Consider

What communities have you been a part of, and how have they helped you transform?

Can you recall a time in your life when you needed to lean on a supportive community?

What kinds of communities have you enjoyed being a member of, and how can you recreate that kind of energy in your community?

What do you want your members to feel, think, have, be, or do?

SpaceX Launch, Cocoa Beach, Florida

"*Fearlessness is not the absence of fear. It's the mastery of fear. It's about getting up one more time than we fall down.*"

— *Arianna Huffington*

CHAPTER 8

Launch Your Community

In April 2021, I had the opportunity to watch a SpaceX launch in
Cocoa Beach, Florida, sitting among a line of lawn chairs across
from the Kennedy Space Center's launch pad. The event was merely
a moment of time. If you blinked, you might have missed it. Even so,
it was thrilling! It was worth the effort to get there, not to mention
for this marvel to happen at all.

To have a clear shot of the space launch (although it just looked
like a beam of light), I planned to park alongside the road. To nab
a spot the night before, I headed to the Merritt Island National
Wildlife Refuge outside the space center. By four in the morning,
there were crowds lined up along the road. We all had our stories,
and we'd collectively spent hours, weeks, and months preparing
to get there.

That's right. A lot goes into the few moments of a launch. In
this chapter, we'll talk about how to set yourself up for a successful community launch. You may be feeling overwhelmed, even if
you've found more clarity in your launch plan. I hope you have! No
worries, though. The resources available in this section will put you
on the path to success.

This is about the time most of my clients ask me how much content they need to create prior to charging for an online community. Of course, the answer will depend on your members' needs and wants, along with what you, as host, want to share with them. That said, I hope I can provide a little calm by saying that I believe *no additional content* needs to be created except for your onboarding plan. The onboarding plan will be discussed in more detail in the next chapter.

I recommend clients start with a soft or slow launch and *bring people inside in phases*. The phases will depend on your audience size, program structure, and available resources.

Some call this a beta launch, or even an alpha launch, but all it means is you will segment your audience on a sliding scale from most interested to least interested.

The most interested group will be your ideal members. They've already said they're interested in what you are creating, so they will be a great place to start.

Selling a community idea is about not only convincing a person that they should invest their time, money, and energy, but also asking them to do so for a set amount of time. My recommendation is to ask five to ten of your ideal members to join a structured program that lasts thirty to ninety days. This will be a sufficient window to test your content and structure, as well as to gain insights on member experience.

Step 1: Learn the Phases of a Launch

When I revamped my own community, I invited five community builders to a ninety-day mastermind program during which we met on Zoom every other Friday. I spoke with each participant individually and shared the structure I'd created for the group. In return for *free* participation in this custom experience, which I was dedicating *my time to cultivating*, they would provide me feedback.

This, in turn, would allow me to decide how to relaunch the community after my failed attempt the previous year.

The structure of the mastermind included weekly and monthly webinars on themes they would vote on. At the conclusion of the program, each member would share their own launch or relaunch plan during a growth seat to receive honest feedback and ideas. Because my outcome was the same as theirs, I also participated as the mastermind, and yes, their feedback helped me refine my own launch plan.

The first steps I took:

1. I reached out to every single person who had ever booked a discovery call with me to let them know I was offering a community specifically for new community builders and wanted to share it with them.
2. I became more active in telling potential clients about the community and offering them a way to stay informed with an email newsletter.
3. I developed a content plan for the website that included information as to how someone would benefit from joining the community. I also created a sales page to increase views of my landing page.

A month after completing this mastermind, I opened the doors for real. Thanks to the outreach I'd already done, I had a few members ready to go. I didn't have any content inside except for some blog articles, but I *did* offer a call with each member when they joined to learn more about their needs.

Phase 1: Pre Launch

The prelaunch phase is when you are planning your events, preparing promotional materials, scheduling tasks, creating content, cultivating partnerships, building relationships, writing content for emails, engaging on social media, and securing conversations on podcasts, radio, television, and news outlets.

This is the most important phase in your launch, and it's the phase on which you want to spend the most time because it will streamline the rest of your launch. Set yourself up for success by creating a launch plan that fits your needs and let go of the expectation for everything to be perfect.

A few ways to build relationships with potential members is by attending networking events, communicating updates with your email subscribers, and sharing your community-building journey with your followers.

Phase 2: Launch

You now have a waitlist, audience, beta members, or email list of people you've been talking to about the community for a while. Now begins the actual launch period when you promote your content, share your offer, and connect with your partners, members, and customers. This also includes onboarding new members by tagging and engaging with them. You will want to make sure you have an onboarding plan (in the next chapter) and that members understand what you are offering. If it is a twelve-week course, be clear about the expected outcomes.

When you provide a subscription-based membership, either month-to-month or annual, make sure you give your members the details of the benefits and features.

Monthly memberships require you to provide constant content or give members a transformational journey which they can easily envision for themselves. I often help clients understand and communicate differences between features and benefits.

Benefits are the outcomes the member experiences:

☆ A community that offers a coaching program to help female founders lose weight can provide the benefits that members

will feel more energetic, more comfortable in their bodies, and more confident in their ability to lead without fear of shame.
* A community that offers a twelve-week course for new homeowners about the do's and don'ts of home remodeling can provide the benefits that members will know how to select the right professionals, determine if the rates they charge are fair, and decide if a project is something they want to do themselves.
* A community that offers monthly networking calls for busy executives in technology offers the benefit of improved communication with their peers in one place and a growth mindset.

Features are what the product or service provides to the members:

* The community that offers a coaching program to help female founders lose weight might feature live calls, an interactive chat channel, or coaching group calls.
* The community that offers a twelve-week course for new homeowners might feature weekly videos, live workshops, course webinars, worksheets, templates, or demonstrations.
* The community that offers a monthly networking call for busy executives in technology might feature the ability to connect to peers who share the same challenges and struggles, as well as offer solutions and resources.

Phase 3: Post Launch

The post launch experience is all about making sure your members adopt the platform you've selected. There is nothing more important than onboarding, which is what we will talk about in the next chapter!

LAUNCH PLAN EXAMPLE (FROM THE FIND CALM HERE COMMUNITY)

April 26–30

1. Create marketing content, including copy, graphics, logos, and images.
2. Set up a new network, with benefits, on the community platform.
3. Write an invitation email to send to leads.

May 10–21

1. Personally reach out to current FCH Members (twenty) to ask them if they want to stay, now that the community membership is shifting from *free to paid*.

May 28

1. Create the community content calendar with themes.
2. Host a monthly call with current members to update them on the changes.

May 24–30

1. Send an invitation to the leads list informing them of the new community structure and the benefits of becoming a member.

May 30

1. Announce the launch on my podcast.
2. Share the launch date on social media and through the email newsletter.

June 20

1. Official launch date! Kick off with a welcome party for all members of the community!

Step 2: Create a Vision for Your Launch

Depending on the nature of your community, *give yourself about two to three months* from vision to launch to avoid feeling overwhelmed. It's important that you proceed with caution and put your health, family, and personal needs before your launch. Don't sacrifice your self-care or self-esteem for anything or anyone.

Next, identify any personal commitments that might take up more time than your usual schedule allows. This may include trips you've planned. Do not plan a launch the same week you fly to Hawaii! Yes, I had a client tell me that was her plan, and yes, she was stressed about it. No, she didn't have a team. Also check with family and friends to see if there's anything that isn't on your calendar yet but will be.

Consider the number of hours each week you can dedicate to this project and block off the nonnegotiable hours in your calendar for community building. Set yourself up for success by creating a unique process for managing each phase of your launch. This doesn't mean you need to learn a lot of new technology. Keep it simple and make it easy to keep track of your progress.

Step 3: Designate Your Tech Tools

Technology tools help community builders organize, schedule, plan, and create content. There are also tools to manage the daily, weekly, and monthly tasks inside your community.

COMMUNITY-BUILDING TECH TOOLS

Beginner: If you're a new community host who is currently clarifying your community structure, your goal is to keep costs to a minimum until your community generates revenue. You'll need:

☆ An email address to invite people to your community with the ability to organize contacts and set reminders.
☆ Digital storage to organize and house online files.

☆ Software to schedule virtual meetings, create forms
  and surveys, organize data, and manage your marketing
  campaigns.
☆ A marketing and promotional tool or person to create
  branding and graphics for your community and share
  with social media.

Intermediate: If you're a community host who's opened the
doors to a small group of people inside your network, you'll want
to grow your community by customizing a strategy to help you
manage your network. You'll need:

☆ A project and task management software to systematize
  your workflow.
☆ A contact management system that can keep track of
  leads, paid members, billing, invoicing, and automat-
  ing forms.
☆ A scheduling application that allows you to share your
  calendar with others for collaborations, onboarding sessions, and networking meetings.
☆ Video software to share recordings of live events and promote your live network, offerings, services, or products.

Advanced: If you have a highly engaged community full of members who are all contributing content, creating conversations, and
inviting others to join, you're in a great place! You need support
with automation, email campaigns, content creation, and product
development. You'll need:

☆ A way to organize into a roadmap the many ideas you
  have for new features and benefits for your product and
  service releases.
☆ Automation of tasks and communication between you
  and your members.

☆ Email marketing, onboarding sequences, and a list-building strategy.

A few examples of tech tools include:

☆ Google email lets you send invitations to your members, organize contacts, and create templates.
☆ Trello, a project-management tool, offers you the ability to manage your community launch plan by visually organizing, scheduling, and assigning tasks to yourself and, if applicable, your team.
☆ Google Drive for data management allows you to store your content and share it with collaborators, partners, and support staff, so all your resources are in one place.
☆ Google Docs for content creation permits your content to be shared with others and updated over time. It's a "living document" that can be accessed anywhere and is backed up to Google Drive.

The above technology tools are for beginners as I don't see a need for new community builders to be very technology savvy. As we've discussed in earlier chapters, it's more about building connections than systems.

I would encourage you to do some research and find the best fit for your community before instructing members on how you'll be communicating with them. If you aren't sure about what the members of your community want, ask them! It is always best to validate your tools and methods before diving in too deep.

Ask this in the form of a poll: How can my community best stay in conversation with you?

1. Send me an email to remind me of community updates and new features.
2. Send me text or mobile notifications from an app.

3. Send me direct messages through the community platform.
4. Send me a calendar invitation for any events or updates.
5. Post your updates on social media because that's where I spend my time.

Data Collection and Organization

As a business owner and host of this community, you will need to find a home for the content you create. I would recommend having a backup system for yourself where you keep files, photos, marketing materials, and reusable copy. This includes things like your "About Us" description, vision statement, and community onboarding materials. If you don't know how to organize your data, first think about how you prefer to collect and use it.

1. Surveys and spreadsheets can help organize data in one place. I usually recommend doing a survey once per quarter (or at least twice a year). This practice keeps you on the pulse of members and lets you know which features and offers appeal to them.
2. Google Drive keeps your images and notes in one place. I recommend creating content in external documents before placing it on your community platform, so you have a record of it should anything happen with that platform provider.
3. Creating a process for your community content workflow can be useful for deciding on new products, features, ideas, and services or reflecting on past projects.

Step 4: Plan Your Content and Experiences

As you plan your experiences, don't become caught up in thinking you need piles of content. In fact, it can be as simple as identifying the content your members consume the most. Start your content strategy by identifying the type of content (articles, links, videos, interactive events) they'll need along their journey. Based on member feedback, determine how frequently they actually use each medium.

Many hosts believe they need to post every day or even several times a day. If you aren't sure if your content is helpful, ask! What I've found is it really depends on your community members' engagement and interaction on the platform. If members are really interested in your content, they will ask for more. Let your idea juices start flowing by exploring the following three content examples.

Example 1—Membership with a Course Structure: Let's say you've identified that your members enjoy the biweekly office hours that happen between your live program or on-demand video content. Create opportunities for members to engage with each other a total of three to five times per week, as follows:

1. First and third Mondays: Conduct office hours. This could be a one-hour "ask me anything" session.
2. Second and fourth Wednesdays: Ask a question about their progress and encourage them to post in the community forum. "How is this week's challenge going for you? What have you learned? How are you implementing this?"
3. First and third Fridays: Post an article or resource to support what members are working on.
4. Second and fourth Mondays: Host a coworking or networking session.

Example 2—Membership with Cohort Structure: Assume you've identified that your members enjoy connecting with the larger community once per month during a workshop, then meeting weekly in smaller cohorts.

1. Monthly: Provide a workshop on a topic that can be helpful for all members.

2. Weekly: Post an article or resource. Provide a poll or other post to encourage habitual engagement.
3. Community Collaboration: Host an event where people can meet each other and welcome new members as a group. Make these fun and interactive; they don't have to include learning.

Example 3—Community Membership Structure: You have identified that your members are in different stages, so you want to offer them different tools, resources, and support. To do this, you are going to provide several ways for members to connect with you and each other.

1. Weekly or biweekly: Host an "ask me anything" or office hours.
2. Weekly on Monday, Wednesday, or Friday: Ask members to share challenges or wins and offer feedback and support for each other.
3. Weekly on Tuesday: Offer pro-tips to help members save time, money, or both. Consider creating a theme around the tips, such as "Tech Tuesday."
4. Daily: If you have an active group, or you are trying to build habits together, offer a daily workout, yoga, or guided meditation to build accountability and connection.

Once you have an idea of the content you want to share, you can set aside time to put it all together. If possible, schedule a month in advance, so you build in time to develop the next month's plan. If you find yourself behind, rethink your plan. Ask yourself which components aren't necessary and simplify.

Chapter Snapshot

☆ Give yourself about two to three months from vision to launch, depending on the nature of your community.

☆ Consider how many hours you can dedicate to this project each week and block off the nonnegotiable hours on your calendar for community building.

☆ Start with your community content strategy by identifying the type of content (articles, links, videos, interactive events) and the frequency, based on your members' needs and feedback.

Action Items

☆ Create your pre launch, launch, and post launch plan.

Questions to Consider

What is a realistic timeframe for you to connect with potential members for discovery calls?

Where do you want to be in six months or a year from now? Be sure to focus on your community strategy.

What can you let go of to move forward with your set launch plan?

Petrified Forest National Park, Arizona

"Without leaps of imagination or dreaming, we lose the excitement of possibilities. Dreaming, after all, is a form of planning."

— Gloria Steinem

CHAPTER 9

Onboard Your Members

When I was visiting Arizona's Petrified Forest National Park in 2019, I was fascinated by the winding paths that snake through the woods. I wanted to take shots of the incredible views, but I didn't know where the best spots were, much less how to access them quickly. It would have been nice to have a roadmap!

When a new member joins your community, make sure they don't feel like I did at that park. Onboarding is an important task; getting it right will ensure your members feel welcomed and set up for success from the start. It sets the tone for how they'll navigate and participate in your community to build relationships. I can state this with confidence after working with so many new community builders, as onboarding is the thing they ask about the most.

When you have your launch plan, and you're ready to invite members in, make sure you have a system that works for you and them.

I've hosted several webinars and workshops about community onboarding. The strategies don't tend to change much, but there are always new tools. As such, try not to become caught up on software. I assure you it's not as important as the five factors below, which are imperative in any community onboarding plan.

Five Community Onboarding Elements

When clients reach out to me to build a new community, it is usually the week before they launch, and they ask me how to onboard their members. The problem with this is that they no longer have time to build a member journey map or the guide which tells their members how they can navigate within your community.

Many new community builders assume that once they open their community, members will instantly know what to do or where to go. Maybe they will explore the community and become curious about events, courses, or programs, but they will most likely only have a few spare moments to find out if this is a place where they want to spend time. Most of the work you'll do to convince them they belong in your community happens long before they are inside.

In the last chapter, we discussed how, when building an audience, it is important to tell people your community's purpose. When members are inside, though, you still have to remind them what this place is and why they belong there. Members will also need to know if they are allowed to share photos or personal information, and they will want to know who is in this space with them.

The most important goal of the onboarding process is to encourage members onto the platform and into conversation with each other. If they don't know other members, they may not come back unless it's for a specific course or a program.

Ultimately, you'll need to make sure you answer all of their questions and welcome them with a feeling of belonging, a guide to tell them where to go, and a plan for the future, so they know what to expect and how to participate. This can be accomplished by following the five community onboarding elements laid out below. In the next sections, I'll explain different methods to implement each one.

☆ What's here: Clearly explain what's included in this space.
☆ Connection: Elevate members who show up consistently.
☆ What's in it for them: Tell them how your community relates to their problem.
☆ Sense of belonging: Make sure members know they are in the "right place."
☆ Make it safe: Inform members what's allowed and what isn't. Community guidelines provide them with expectations about how to participate.

A Clear Message

The biggest mistake new community builders make is moving too fast, too soon. When hosts skip setting up an onboarding process, they risk losing members from the start. Even though *you* need to be thoughtful about onboarding, the process should feel quick and easy for each new member. An invitation to join the community should be short and sweet, and any message you share should have a clear action step.

Recently, I spent several hours training on a new software for hosting communities. It took me a long time to figure out where things were, how to sign up for live sessions, and how to locate relevant documents. The experience wasn't fun, and at times it was even stressful. I eventually found what I was looking for, but most people won't spend as many hours figuring things out, unless it's for a job.

The best way to design an onboarding process is to first receive feedback from your existing members about their experience when they joined. Was it easy? Fun? Stressful? Be specific and find the places members became stuck.

A CLEAR MESSAGE CAN BE DEFINED IN A FEW STEPS

1. Tell the member what the community is all about and why they are a part of it.
2. Give them the steps to join in an easy-to-implement format.
3. Provide a few ways to learn about what they can do inside the community, including written descriptions, screenshots, and quick video or audio how-tos.
4. Provide the rules, expectations, and guidelines to ensure they feel confident in their contributions.

Offer a Variety of Ways to Invite Members In

Thanks to ever-changing technology, it can be difficult to know the best way to communicate with new members. The methods will differ depending on your community's structure, the devices involved, and your team's familiarity with technology. This is why it's good to first ask your existing members about their experience and make changes based on their feedback.

My experience, and that of my clients, reveals that the platform you choose makes a major difference in the onboarding experience. Remember, you must also factor in the devices your audience uses. If your members are primarily downloading an app on their mobile devices to access the platform, it will be a totally different experience than using a desktop or tablet. If you know most members are desktop users, then your onboarding should match this experience. Note: If it would suit most of your members, you may choose to recommend one kind of device over another, but make sure you communicate this clearly at every stage.

THE VIDEO WALKTHROUGH—VERBAL AND AUDITORY LEARNERS

You can create a video that walks members through how to navigate the community. Show them the content, explain how they can connect, and discuss why they'll want to participate in events. Let them know how to consume and create content as well. This will allow them to learn on their own time whenever they are able to access the tutorial. No matter what you do, keep these videos short and easy to understand.

ORIENTATION PACKET—VISUAL, SOLITARY, AND LOGICAL LEARNERS

Over the years, I've created packets that provide photos, screenshots, and step-by-step instructions on where to go, what to do, and how to connect. The packet can be sent ahead of your kickoff call, and you can invite them into the community a few days early to make sure they can access everything they need.

LEARN BY DOING—PHYSICAL AND SOCIAL LEARNERS

You can create an event, course, or challenge that encourages them to upload a profile photo, write an introduction, or connect in another way. Through social events such as a welcome party or orientation, you can introduce your network members to one another. These are great ways to connect your members right from the start, and you may be surprised by the lasting bonds sparked by meaningful experiences such as these.

CONCIERGE—SOLITARY, VERBAL, AND AUDITORY LEARNERS

You can personally welcome each new member via phone, video, email, or text. This takes time to do on your part, but high-touch experiences justify a higher-priced membership. When people need active support, personalized options provide the chance to build deep relationships. This can be effective when your participants are in different stages or prefer small, trusted cohorts.

Onboarding Prompts to Encourage Your Members

Creating a few prompts inside your community can help encourage members to join conversations. In many platforms, using an "at sign" (@) to tag a member alerts the individual directly.

Using prompts, invite members to get to know each other. Here are a few examples:

* ☆ Let's get to know each other! Please add a fun photo to your profile and share the story behind it!
* ☆ Who's here? Introduce yourself and share one thing you'd like to give and one thing that you need from us.
* ☆ What brought you here?
* ☆ What are you most excited about?
* ☆ Who will be the first to complete their profile? The winner will hold the title of "Community Superstar" for one month.

Let members know how to set up (and turn off) notifications, as well as where they can manage their dashboard. Here is an example:

* ☆ We are so excited you've joined us! We want to make sure you don't miss a thing, but we know a lot of notifications can be annoying. We recommend you select "Daily Digest," so you receive only one email each day to keep updated on the community.

Encourage members to discover each other as well:

* ☆ We are super excited that [@ name of member] has joined. We know [what you know about that person], and I know that [name of another member] may also have [common interest, same role, similar location].

☆ Check out the newest members in the directory [and explain how to access]! Click "Follow," so you are updated when they post.

Community Guidelines

When bringing new members into the community, you'll want to make sure they know it's a space where they can share freely, without judgment or harassment. To ensure safety and privacy for all in your community, you'll need to use clear language to describe what is and is not acceptable.

It is important to let members know that any information they share will be secure and will not be used without their permission. Many countries and states have differing privacy laws, so check that you are compliant with your local regulations. Plan to have a privacy policy, community guidelines, and terms and conditions that fit your business and community structure. Make sure to have your legal team review your policies to ensure they are enforceable and, if necessary, will hold up in court.

Having an area for community guidelines is vital to any community. Your guidelines should include expectations for privacy and conduct, as well as any legal terms and conditions.

Here are a few examples of language you may want to include in your community guidelines:

Due to the private nature of this community and its content, all images, graphics, and written, audio, and video content are owned by [Host/Organization Name]. The following guidelines are in place to ensure privacy and safe dialogue for all members.

1. This is a professional community. Members are expected to communicate in a manner that respects each person's individuality and right to express themselves. [State your specific expectations]

2. No political, religious, or other non relevant conversations will be tolerated. Any member who violates this rule will be asked to remove the content. [Adjust this depending on your community content, context, and focus.]

3. Members are encouraged to post positive, encouraging content. This space assumes every member is on their own journey and has their own context. Member comments are intended to encourage other members, not solve problems for them. [Customize this for your member content and community focus.]

4. If a member posts content that doesn't fit with these guidelines, the member will be warned once. If the member repeats this behavior, the member will be removed. [Customize this to clarify what is acceptable and what isn't.]

5. Members are encouraged to post questions or comments for moderators or fellow members in the "Topics" area. They may also add links to resources such as articles or videos. [Customize this for your content and member expectations.]

6. Members are encouraged to connect with each other in the following ways:
   a. Commenting in the activity feed
   b. Responding to content provided by the host or other members
   c. Sending messages through group messaging

Connection and Belonging

One of the most valuable tasks of a community host is effectively communicating with members. Many new community builders make the mistake of assuming members will connect organically, but this doesn't typically happen. On the contrary, it's your responsibility to tell people how you want them to show up and model it for them within the space. Members need a guide to help them know who's there and why they should connect.

To ensure you establish a strong sense of belonging, you'll need to clarify what the members have in common. Lay out how they can support each other through challenges. For example, you may be running a learning community where members are at different stages of development—beginner, intermediate, and advanced. If mentorship is something your community encourages, consider establishing a clear way for advanced members to share their experiences with beginners. Remind them it's not a member's job to solve others' problems, rather to encourage growth and learning.

If your community is large, consider establishing topic groups within the platform, so members can bond over shared interests. Encourage members to fill out their profiles. This isn't something they'll do on their own; you need to tell them it's an option that will enhance their experience.

Incorporate ways for members to get to know each other and foster relationships over time. This might be during events with paired breakout sessions or by seeding discussions in topical groups.

Chapter Snapshot

☆ Ask the members to describe their experience. Was it easy? Fun? Stressful? Be specific and find the places members become stuck.

☆ Each invitation to join the community needs to be short, simple, and have a clear action step.

☆ Connection and belonging are important aspects in the onboarding process and will take time to cultivate. Make intentional connections with members who have similar values, interests, professional roles, or live in the same regions.

Action Items

1. Identify how your members will be invited to join the community and the device they'll use to access it.
2. Ask your existing members about their onboarding experience and identify their recommendations for how you might improve it.
3. Outline what members receive when they join your community. Ask them how they want to get the most out of their membership.

Questions to Consider

How will members be joining and when?

What will they do when they enter your space and in what order?

How will you connect them to one another?

SECTION 4:

Community Retention, Growth, and Maintenance

Newport, Rhode Island

"Choose actions that show the customer that they matter."
— *Marilyn Suttle*

CHAPTER 10

Keep Members Coming Back

My own life has been transformed by well-run communities. I know firsthand the value of being a member of a thriving community. As a journalist-turned-podcaster, I've investigated what makes online communities flourish. Since starting my journey, I've reached out to and interviewed over 100 experts, colleagues, and leaders who have been building online communities for years, even decades. I always ask them to share what has worked as they have built, launched, and grown their online communities. I'm fascinated to discover what brings members back again and again. In this chapter, I'll share my key findings from interviews with experts who have built thriving communities.

What Makes a Community Successful as a Business?

Rosie Sherry has been in the community-building space since 2006 when she started connecting with others during meetups. In 2010, she founded a coworking space while working as a software tester. During her first few years in this role, she tested software for fun. Over time, she developed skills that she turned into a community-focused business. Rosie built the Ministry of Testing community from the ground up. At the time of our interview, her community had brought in more than seven figures and had over 75,000 members. Rosie has also launched Indie Hackers, a community of over 32,000 creators, where she hosts events.

Rosie's business revenue includes event and membership dues, in addition to sponsorships. The income enabled her to hire a team that manages the day-to-day operations. When we spoke, her communities had run without her daily oversight for more than three years, yet they were the projects she was most proud of building. She's also shared that eighty percent of her team was recruited from the community, so they've known the value and purpose from the start. They have a passion for helping their fellow community members to not simply survive, but also thrive.

When she stepped back from the operations of Indie Hackers, Rosie challenged herself to build, launch, and grow yet another online community. "In the beginning, I had doubts that I could do it again, but I realized the transferable skills I've already got, and I know what I'm doing! I've done it before!"

She had seen other community builders struggle after skipping the discovery phase, so she knew she needed to find validation before committing to her new concept.

Once Rosie realized she loved community building, she kept going and developed more! Now, she has several spaces where she helps fellow creators, founders, and community builders. One is The Independent Community, a private Slack channel to ask Rosie anything, so long as they participate in the community in return. If new members fail to engage within their first six months, she boots them out.

She also offers Lurk as a Service (LaaS), which provides organizations with monthly consulting services. This evolved from her previous role as the founder and community executive officer at Rosieland, where she hosted ticketed events. Originally, this venture brought in seventy percent of her revenue, largely through in-person meetings. After the pandemic, she added online courses, curated community content, and offered consulting services. Rosie makes the case that putting people first is the key to building successful communities:

> *Finding a balance between the needs of the members, aligning them with the business values and goals. It is important to keep members happy, but increasingly, I am trying to think of ways that the business can thrive while bringing value to the community. If we (community builders) put people at the heart of what we build, this is the way to become successful.*

She says that community builders who aren't confident can find it challenging to make decisions and take action. Rosie said she focuses on talking to members individually to learn about their needs but always makes decisions with the business and heart of the membership in mind.

Strategies for Getting and Keeping Your Most Valuable People

Adrian Speyer, author of *The Accidental Community Manager,* has over a decade of experience in the community industry. At the time of our interview, he was head of community at Higher Logic Vanilla, a SaaS community platform. Adrian has worked with top brands to teach community builders best practices and effective frameworks for impacting organizational goals.

On "Episode 96: Becoming an Accidental Community Manager with Adrian Speyer" of *The Community Strategy Podcast,* Adrian talks

about what leads to a successful B2B Community. "The return on investment for communities is a lot more than just increased revenue; it could be increasing brand awareness or improving the customer experience."

As Adrian points out, any community professional is going to make mistakes, but the key is to learn from them, while staying connected to your members. The members are your "most valuable people," he says, so it's your job to consistently provide them with value. He reiterates that community building takes care and intention, and success depends on developing a strategy related to the community's goals, values, and mission.

Céline Riemenschneider is the community lead for the German Canva Creator Community, which supports over 850,000 designers across thirty-seven private communities. Under Céline's leadership, artists based in Germany create localized designs for Canva customers to fill the growing number of categories.

In running this community, Céline reviews its data to inform Canva of the latest successes and challenges for these German creators. Céline says that the key elements to a successful community for Canva include workshops, networking, member-led and inspired events, and improved search engine optimization to support creators from beginner to advanced.

> *After our workshops, we get so much great feedback from members who tell us that the training was so valuable and that they are excited to try what they've learned. Sometimes it's easy to forget about their experience, and it's a great reminder to be grateful to the members who develop skills and learn new things with the support of the community.*

From Publishing to Community Powerhouse: How a CEO Used Community to Shift her Magazine into a Connection Company

What started with a whisper and a few women connecting in 2012 has turned into a 3,500-member community of women supporting each other to be more of themselves. Shannon Crotty, founder and

CEO of Polka Dot Powerhouse, started a local women's magazine in Wisconsin. After moving to the area and not knowing many people, she knew she needed a sisterhood.

Two years earlier, her sister, Tina, passed away. One day, while sitting in her car, missing her sister dearly, she said, "Tina, I need your help and guidance." Suddenly, the name "Polka Dot Power-house" came to Shannon, and a movement was born.

Since then, the "Dot Sisters," as they are called, have connected in meetings worldwide, in chapters from the United States, Canada, and the United Kingdom. I learned about them a while ago, but it wasn't until a friend invited me to attend a local chapter that I discovered how valuable this group of women is for my life.

Now, with over eighty chapters in the U.S. and Canada, and over 3,500 members, this amazing community has grown, over a decade, to become a truly powerful place to find a supportive group of women who aren't interested in pretending to be someone else.

"When asked about my goals, I tell people that I'm not trying to reach a specific number of members, but it's about aligning the vision and focusing on the mission. I want to ensure we are giving the members a good experience," Shannon said.

After the story Shannon shared, and with many women holding napkins from tears about her journey and challenges, I asked her the question I'm facing right now, "How do you keep going?"

What Shannon said was so powerful.

> *If you can trust the distance of light provided by car head-lights (approximately 300 feet) to shine a path in front of you, you will be shown the next steps, but when it's time, and when there is a reason. Keep going; you can't deal with challenges unless they are right in front of you. Don't worry about the next month or year; worry about the next few hours, days, or weeks.*

Polka Dot Powerhouse's vision is to reach every woman who needs support when needed and understand that not all women will need their help, and they aren't a fit for every woman. Shannon is the CEO and believes it's essential for the CEO to understand the mission and vision of the community. Since this community is the business, that's the core objective—to keep memberships and encourage growth. "I wanted to be a great CEO, and if a CEO can't visit with their members, it isn't a sisterhood!"

I have enjoyed the smaller group that the evening meetings tend to host, which offers a cozy atmosphere. It helps that we have a fantastic director, Jackie Orth. She has been a welcoming host from the beginning of my journey with the Polka Dot Powerhouse Lancaster Chapter.

Chapter Snapshot

☆ Rosie has spent twelve years building successful communities by understanding the member's experience. She first started a community for fun and turned that into a seven-figure business.

☆ Adrian says the key to retention is knowing your most valuable people' and consistently providing them with value.

☆ Céline reviews the community data to inform Canva of the latest successes and challenges within the community.

Action Items

1. Set aside time to identify your community's most valuable people and make sure you thank them for their contributions.
2. Schedule check-ups with community members monthly, quarterly, or annually.
3. Ask community members to share their current challenges. Gather feedback and any new ideas they bring.

Questions to Consider

How often will my community manager or team check on member retention?

How does my community define success?

When will we make decisions about the community strategy?

Rocky Mountain Arsenal National Wildlife Refuge, Denver, Colorado

"I don't believe in failure. It is not a failure if you enjoy the process."

— *Oprah Winfrey*

CHAPTER 11

Grow Your Membership

It takes about three years to see an online community really thrive. In past chapters, I shared the importance of asking your members what kind of support they need and how the community can benefit them. If you're ready to see your community grow significantly, the same concept applies. If your community already has solid content, connections, and interactions, this chapter can especially help you grow.

When thinking about growth, most community professionals rely on data to measure what's working, so they can adjust their strategy for continued growth. While data is an effective resource, it's important to remember that *people* are the reason a community exists. It can be challenging, but make sure you don't become stuck on the numbers. In this chapter, I'll offer a few ways to use data to reach desired business outcomes, and we'll cover how to define growth metrics and inform decisions.

Any community needs to be healthy to grow, but what, exactly, defines "health"? There's no single answer, but there are patterns you can seek. Once you've had a community for six months or more, you can begin collecting information about the content you are providing and review members' commitment, contribution, and activity. You can determine the "health" of your community by reviewing a few *key data points* and comparing them with the community growth plan.

These key data points include:

* Members who have logged into the community.
* Frequency of each member's logins.
* The number of events each community member has attended.
* The most consumed content (videos, articles, posts, or discussions).
* The highest ranking posts based on likes, cheers, and comments.
* The number of courses members have completed.
* The number of times each member has created a post or shared an article, blog, or photo.

The priority for these elements will depend on your community structure but be aware that not all data holds the same value. For example, social-media metrics are sometimes called "vanity" metrics, because they don't reflect actual engagement. Knowing someone "saw" a piece of content is not as valuable as knowing they contributed to a comment thread, for instance.

There are a few formulas that help community professionals measure data for healthy community outcomes.

Community Champions

Community champions are your core members who share their energy, time, and resources. Community champions can be members who volunteer to lead coworking sessions, encourage new members to participate, comment on posts, or share their knowledge. It's important to acknowledge community champions through shout-outs. Recognize them with things such as badges or opportunities to share with the community, showing other members they are trusted leaders. They can help you grow your community by encouraging engagement, recruiting new members, and offering ideas for experiences.

What's Best for Them?

Many new community builders waste valuable energy focusing on lower-priority metrics, such as a platform's ambassador program. A better way to spend your time is to understand what's best for the members. It might be exciting to have active and highly engaged members, but asking them to be ambassadors from the very beginning doesn't serve them well. They haven't solidified their own experiences yet, so they haven't completely bought in. Especially important in the first one to three years, your primary goal is to develop a core culture that suits their needs.

By understanding what's best for them and providing it, you'll give your members a better experience. Only after undergoing their own transformation will they want to tell others about it. If you're implementing an ambassador program, don't ask members to participate unless you've confirmed you've met their needs.

You can confirm what's best through surveys, polls, and interviews. As you consistently do this, you'll start to identify your key champions over time. Once you have a sense of who they are, initiate a conversation with them. If you sense they are fired up about your offering and want to share it, it might be a suitable time for an ambassador program. Even then, be thoughtful about making it worth their while.

Ask Them

Did I say that again? Yes. Asking your community champions how *they* want to share the community should come before creating any kind of advocacy program. If you are considering offering a referral, rewards, or affiliate program, ask the members what benefits they'd want besides monetary rewards. Members will tell friends and family about the community because it helped them solve a problem. If you've provided a trusted place to explore topics about which they are passionate, they'll often *want* to help you expand the community.

Slow Growth is Better Growth

When I work with clients to launch a community, I always recommend a phased approach. The same goes for growing the community. It takes intentional action to connect members over time. The best growth strategy is to have an amazing onboarding process, provide great resources, and offer a unique member experience that keeps them coming back. If you serve more than one type of member, I recommend focusing on one group at a time.

Set a goal for growth within your community. Decide how many active members you'd like to have. When you reach that goal, invite more people in and encourage them to tell others. Trying to build out too many spaces within a community is where a lot of problems start to occur.

For example, say you are viewing a website, and you see a few navigation links at the top; this is how you can think about organizing a community. Some community builders think they should have topic areas or spaces for topical conversations to take place, but that rarely works unless you have a very large community.

When starting small, you need to think about members entering your community as if they were exploring a website. What are the features you *need*? You need an events area to host your meetups, a space for members to interact, and a place to organize resources and information.

There was once a feature on the Mighty Networks platform called "Topics." The feature has changed with the updates to the platform and is now called "Spaces," but the new design caused a lot of confusion for customers.

Many customers had more than a few community topics, but when the feature was removed, they didn't know how to organize their content. Many customers turned their topics into a "Space," but this did not work for everyone. By speaking with them, I've learned that having too many choices leads members to leave.

I encourage you to have a strategy for each space you create no matter what platform you decide to use. The terminology might change, but the concept is the same. How will your members know where to connect, share, chat, or communicate?

Think about the following questions:

* ☆ What's the purpose of this space?
* ☆ What is included?
* ☆ Who will watch over or maintain it?
* ☆ What is your strategy for this space?

They Matter

Of course, every member is a human being. Keep in mind that each person has a full life with various responsibilities, possibly including family, kids, work, commutes, conferences, health challenges, doctor appointments, and travel plans. Each person has come to your community for a reason. The more you know why they decided to join and what their lives are like, the better you'll understand their participation.

Whether they show up constantly or sporadically, they have a reason. Most times, a personal event has changed their daily life; they may need time to get back to their normal activities. Think about members when they are gone and check in on them. If they've had health concerns, community members can come together and send a card. They matter! The more you show you care, the more valued they will feel. This is the best way you can encourage them to show up again and share their experiences with their network.

Community Metrics Inform Leadership Decisions

Metrics give data to an organization's leadership that aid in decision making. Richard Millington, author of *Buzzing Communities: How to Build Bigger, Better, and More Active Online Communities*, explains the importance of strategic analysis. "It's like a puzzle . . . data, business goals, metrics . . . if you don't get these things to work together, a community will struggle."

From "Episode 93: Community Strategy that utilizes data with Richard Millington":

During my interview with Richard on *The Community Strategy Podcast*, he shared that each organization deals with metrics in different ways. There's no "right" way to measure success for an online community, he pointed out, but metrics do show impact. Whatever measurements you track, you need to make sure the results reflect your overall goals and mission. This can only be achieved long-term, he says, if you provide enough value to encourage highly active members.

"The goal of the inception stage is to achieve critical mass by cultivating a small group of highly active members in the community," he explains. "This group becomes the foundation upon which to build the community. Unless a small, active, group is established, it is impossible to develop a successful long-term community."

Chapter Snapshot

* ☆ Community "health" is defined as knowing your community goals and aligning them with the community members' experiences.
* ☆ Once you've had a community for six months, you can begin to collect information about the provided content and review members' commitment, contribution, and activity.
* ☆ Community growth includes these core concepts: community champions, what's best for them, ask them, slow growth, and they matter.
* ☆ There's no "right" way to measure success for an online community.

Action Items

1. Make a list of the most important metrics for your organization.
2. Focus on these for the next thirty, sixty, or ninety days.
3. Set a few SMART goals for the metrics you've chosen.

What metrics are most important for your community's growth?

What will help members remember to visit the community?

Who are your community champions right now?

How can you show your champions you appreciate them?

Italian Lake, Harrisburg, Pennsylvania

"Just say yes . . . and you'll figure it out afterwards."
— *Tina Fey*

CHAPTER 12

Maintain Your Community

Back in 2012, well before developing my own community, I went to my first improv comedy show. I had struggled with taking myself too seriously, so when a friend suggested I join her, I was interested to see if it could help me to get rid of my "Debbie Downer" attitude. (And yes, I despise that term.)

The result? I was instantly laughing and realized I wanted to laugh even more, so I started attending monthly shows. Over the years, I became a superfan, attending shows with friends and inviting others along. Three years later, I decided to try improv for myself. I wanted to jump out of my comfort zone, so I signed up for a beginner's class at the Harrisburg Improv Theatre (HIT). I knew back then that I wanted to do some sort of public speaking, but I wasn't sure exactly what that looked like, so improv was a great way to become comfortable with being on stage.

Over time, my confidence, in life and onstage, grew. Six years after that first class, I signed up for a level two class. A year later, I went *way* out of my comfort zone and registered for level three. By that time, I'd built relationships within the improv community in Harrisburg. It was like nothing I'd experienced in my adult life. I instantly felt welcomed. I also felt included, a sensation I hadn't experienced for a long time.

The reason I felt welcomed was because I'd been *invited* to participate. I'd been encouraged to connect with others. Anyone can attend a show or take a class, but this community provided a path to become more involved. Not only was there a path to involvement, but there were also leaders in each class who guided me to participate and engage further. After class, community members went to dinner and had a great meal together. As I discovered, it's hard to beat the feeling of being welcomed by a community of peers.

Years later, a fellow improv friend shared with me that she wanted to shift her existing courses online and wanted my help. Excited by this opportunity, I jumped in to help her make the transition by becoming her community manager. At the time, I had a solid understanding of the technology setup, but the focus of the community, Reiki healing, was unfamiliar to me.

I worked hard to reach out to each member, answer their questions, and guide them through navigation of the community. However, I struggled to connect with them in a deep and meaningful way. Although I cared about their member experience, I didn't share their passion for the subject matter.

What I took away from that experience is that, while I loved and related to my improv friend (the community host), I wasn't a good fit as her community manager. When I speak with clients about hiring a support team, I always recommend starting from within the community. Your members are already interested in the subject, and some have built friendships and partnerships outside the platform. Maybe they even consider other members among some of their best friends. Community members are the best people to help you grow your membership; when you're first starting out, they may even volunteer to help things start moving!

Before Hiring Your First Community Manager

If you need support, I recommend that you document your current processes to manage the community through a standard operating procedure (SOP). If you plan to hire a community manager, they'll need this document as a guide. Many new community professionals will expect to be trained by you or your team.

If you don't yet have an SOP, it's worth your time to set one up. Start by writing out everything you can think of that's required to operate your community. You can perfect the document later. For now, capture anything that comes to mind. Consider the software and the time needed to set up each community space within it. Take notes about tasks to perform within the software, such as logging into your community platform, updating or adding content, and creating events. You should write out everything you currently do or anything you want the community manager to do.

I wish I could tell you an easier way to do this, but it's about getting what you know out of your head. Someone else needs to be able to read, understand, and act from your guidance.

Pro-Tip: You could use artificial intelligence (AI) or voice-recording software to transcribe your SOP for you. Alternatively, you might hire a virtual assistant (VA) to capture your verbal brain dump and turn it into action steps. Remember, this person's job isn't to read your mind. You still need to be heavily involved in the process.

Consider what this community manager will do and how they will best support you. For example, if you run a course, how can they help you gather materials, set up events, or schedule social media promotion posts? The more specific you are about what you need, the easier it will be to find the right person.

The community industry has become a booming field where you can find various kinds of community managers. Some are more operational based, focusing on systems, processes, and efficiency. Other community managers are focused on member experience. These professionals moderate the digital space, ensure members receive what they need, and respond when expectations aren't being met.

So many of my clients want to hire a community manager right at the start of their journey. I did, too. I learned, however, that the decision to hire really depends on the community hosts' individual needs, intentions, challenges, and goals, which will determine when and how to hire a community manager.

Ultimately, it comes down to budget. If you have the financial backing to hire support, then great! If you don't, you'll need to find ways to utilize ambassadors, advocates, volunteers, moderators, and members who want to support the community.

How, When, and Why to Hire a Community Manager

After years of hosting my own community, and as someone who's met dozens of community managers worldwide, I was so excited to offer my services to entrepreneurs as their community manager. I was eager and ready to dive in. Following my first crash-course experience as a community manager, I thought it would be relatively easy to do it again. I was wrong. Very wrong.

I learned that many businesses are still trying to understand how a community professional fits in their organization. Further, many business owners have unrealistic expectations about how much revenue the community will bring in and how quickly. They assume the community will fund the community manager, which may not be the case.

If you are new to community building, you will need to determine a reliable business model. There are *so* many ways this could happen—courses, classes, workshops, retreats—that becoming overwhelmed is a distinct possibility. There's no single way to build an income stream around a community, and figuring out the best model for you and your people will take time. If your community strategy isn't in place and you're not yet generating revenue, you should think long and hard about whether hiring a community manager is necessary.

Pro-Tip: Keep an open mind when thinking about funding the hiring of a community manager. If your community is not generating enough revenue to sustain a team of support, consider how your other business revenue could help support the community.

Even if your revenue stream is reliable, you will need to be strategic when onboarding a new team member. If you are not the sole decision maker, and your leadership struggles to understand why a community is important, it's time to get on the same page. For example, a community manager and a social-media manager aren't the same thing, but to those unfamiliar with how a community functions, the distinction may need to be explained. Be clear that social media is about promotion, sales, and getting leads.

Community management is about building relationships, solving problems, and facilitating a safe space. Many community managers offer technical support to members when problems arise. A good community manager will know many of the members of a community by first name and usually can tell you something about each one. Depending on how active the host is within the community, it may be the *manager* who's the heart and soul of the space. Members should feel comfortable expressing their issues and asking questions when needed.

No matter the platform, a community manager needs to understand the importance of their role. Maybe they handle the daily operations, so the host can focus on the business development and growth strategies.

BEFORE YOU HIRE A COMMUNITY MANAGER
1. Develop an SOP for your community processes.
2. Allocate funds to cover the investment.
3. Make time to train this new person.
4. Prepare a thirty- or sixty-day plan to guide them.

Guidance for New Community Hosts and Managers

I asked several community professionals what they wish they had known when they started out. These experts represent various spaces, including business-to-business and customer communities. Here are their thoughts:

Pat Cooney is a Community Engineer at ProntoForms, a software provider for corporate technicians who work with remote and outside field teams. Pat says, "Always ask questions, and always reach out for help. Remain flexible and be ready, willing, and able to adjust your course as you go. What is true today may not be true in six months, and you need to be agile enough to adjust to shifting realities and targets."

Glory Osiagor is a social media manager and community manager for NNN, an ecosystem that "empowers the Crypto revolution." As Glory points out, "It's okay to feel frustrated and lost; it only means you are one step closer to becoming one of the best community builders because those scaling this niche never had an easy journey."

Matthew Grande, cofounder of Careerage, gives the following advice for new community builders: "Start with twenty-five to thirty people who you can spend time building a relationship with. Don't do any of the technical set up alone; hire someone. Give the founding members the ability to craft their own experience."

Pablo Gonzalez, co-founder of BeTheStage, serves as the community builder show host. He also generated more than $40 million for a single client. He advises, "Don't try to be Superman. Build the Avengers as quickly as possible and share the stage with them. Create a space where you add value and each individual member both receives and adds value at their own capacity or want."

As Jenny Weigle, a strategic consultant for large enterprise companies, points out, knowing the expectations of stakeholders within your organization is vital to success and growth. "I learned how to work with stakeholders in other areas of the company to help them understand the community benefits. Those are skills I had to focus on and build over time. It would have helped to know how to talk to them about their goals and how the community could help to achieve them."

Paul M. Bradley, vice president of Community at Kaplan, advocates approaching the community with curiosity:

> *I really wish I'd known that campaigns didn't need to be perfect to launch, that it's more important to have something out there bringing people together because people don't only collaborate with one another over perfect experiences. I spent nearly a year working on a grand plan for a community that was already launched. When I left, I was disappointed with what I had achieved. I should have just been firing my ideas out there as they came and running with what stuck.*

Robert Maddox, community manager for Delinea, shares the importance of utilizing your personal network. "Start with an internal audit of the company and get to know existing community members before launching a new campaign. As for building my own community or meetup, double down on events to start and build the community and content around those."

Vineet Nandan Gupta, a community strategist and consultant, says, "Community building takes many long hours, beyond the expected, until members treat you as one of them, and that is a thin line to tread a lot of times."

Chapter Snapshot

☆ Have a standard operating procedure (SOP) in place before hiring a community manager and have a good sense of what you'll need before you need it.

☆ Consider what this community manager would do and how they could best support you in your current situation.

☆ Hire from within the community (if possible) as the members already know about the subject manner and have built relationships.

Action Items

1. Write your SOP. Capture everything you do to keep the community running.
2. Identify tasks you don't enjoy doing and seek support as needed.
3. If your budget is tight, identify whether a community manager is important to have right now. If so, craft a plan for funding them or find a volunteer.

Questions to Consider

Determine what kind of community manager you might need by asking yourself what tasks feel overwhelming. Is it technology, behind-the-scenes management, engaging with members?

What steps are involved in operating the community?

Which advice from the experts featured in this chapter most resonated with you?

Skydiving in Colorado, 2019

"To have played and laughed with enthusiasm and sung with exultation; to know even one life has breathed easier because you have lived—this is to have succeeded."
— Bessie Anderson Stanley

Afterward: So, What's Next?

We've come to the end of our journey together, and hopefully you're feeling a bit more confident in your community strategy. I hope my stories and examples have inspired you to think differently, take action, and try something new. With any luck, you'll find success doing something you wouldn't have considered before opening this book.

Whether you're clarifying your concept, preparing to launch, or revamping your current model, I hope I've helped you develop an actionable plan and have energized you to move forward.

On the other hand, you might have concluded that a community isn't something you're ready to build right now. If that's the case, please don't be discouraged. There's nothing wrong with exploring now, so you can build later. As I discovered, even simply being an online community member can be one of the most rewarding experiences.

Work With Me

One of my goals for this book is to let you know you're not alone. If you'd like one-on-one guidance as you plan, launch, or grow your community, I can help! Feel free to email me at Deb@FindCalmHere.com or go to my website, FindCalmHere.com, to schedule a time to talk. I'd love to hear from you!

If you'd like to work with me, there are several ways I can support you.

A strategy session is a ninety-minute virtual call. You will bring your questions and challenges, and we'll workshop them together. Topics are tailored to your unique needs and may include your community concept, strategy, or structure.

Coaching for community hosts, leaders, and managers features weekly meetings where we discuss how to boost your community. This is a one- or three-month commitment and is customized to your needs.

* ☆ Want to workshop your community strategy?
* ☆ Need help refining your launch plan?
* ☆ Want guidance as you develop an onboarding process?
* ☆ Are you seeking advocates or ambassadors?

The topic is up to you, but let's get you moving!

Coaching for new business owners is for those ready to start their entrepreneurial journey. If you're ready to leave a nine-to-five job, it's important to know your strengths, values, and what you bring to the table. As a YouMap® coach, I will help you explore your business ideas and align them with what matters to you. Together, we'll put together a purpose statement you can use for your website, social media, and other areas of promotion.

The Community Consultants Collective is a group for consultants in the community industry. My advisory team and I run this collaborative environment to support you in operating your own consulting business.

If you've picked up this book because you are a fellow community builder, you are welcome to join our meetups on the first Wednesday of each month. Head to www.communityconsultants.life to learn more.

Additional Resources

I invite you to subscribe to the *Find Calm Here Newsletter*. Go to FindCalmHere.com to subscribe. Follow me on LinkedIn to find resources, tools, and tips on building an online community. Visit FindCalmHere.com to view community-building resources, blogs, book reviews, and a list of community books and podcasts. Go to bonus.creator2communitybuilder.com for downloadable resources.

Acknowledgements

Thank you to the Location Indie community, as they inspired me to join and actively participate in an online community for the first time, which led to a life-changing experience, as well as this book!

Thank you to the members who came from the Location Indie community to the Find Calm Here community and partnered and cohosted workshops with me.

Thank you to the Mighty Mastermind members who showed up for me when I needed direction in my life. You gave me the confidence I needed to take the next step into leadership.

Thank you to the many clients who have hired me over the years. Without your financial support, I would not be doing this work or writing this book.

Thank you to the Community Consultants Collective who supported me through this book process and encouraged me when I doubted myself.

Thank you to Todd Nilson for your support and encouragement, as well as for giving me the space and time in my life to write this book.

Thank you to the Creator to Community Builder Crowdfunding campaign supporters for making this book possible!

About the Author

Since 2020, Deb has guided more than sixty entrepreneurs in building, launching, and growing an online community. Her work spans the globe with business leaders in the United States, Mexico, Canada, Europe, Australia, New Zealand, Ireland, Spain, Brazil, and Norway.

Deb works with an organization's leadership in three areas: discovery, strategy, and implementation of an online community. She also provides best practices for organization, digital content management, and tools to keep it simple for both the user experience and the back-end operations. Deb is on the board of the Community Consultants Collective, a group she started in 2021 with fellow consultants who gathered to share resources, expertise, and encouragement.

In addition to her community work, Deb is a published photographic landscape photographer and photojournalist. She graduated from Point Park University with a bachelor's degree in photojournalism and from The Art Institute of Pittsburgh with an associate degree in photography. Deb worked as a writer, photographer, reporter, and editor for newspapers, online publications, and magazines. From 2009 to 2016 Deb's work was featured in Central Pennsylvania print and online publications. She shifted to travel writing in September 2018 and was able to pitch stories in 2020 before the pandemic.

Deb is known in the Central Pennsylvania region for her photographs of the city of Harrisburg. Her large-scale artwork was purchased and is available for view at The Penn Harris Hotel and Convention Center since March 2020.

Because of the global pandemic, plans for an art exhibition were put on hold, and Deb decided to close her photography business to focus on building an online consulting business geared toward helping new community builders.

In 2022, Deb became a certified YouMap® coach, which provides a container for exploring ideas, alignment with values, and a purpose statement with Deb's guidance and over twenty years of her writing experience.

Printed in the USA
CPSIA information can be obtained
at www.ICGtesting.com
LVHW051629250724
786531LV00028B/270

9 798988 816607